Overcoming Shyness and Social Anxiety

Ruth Searle began her career as a nurse and midwife and, although her love of nursing has remained constant, she went on to fulfil her dream of becomin marine biologist. She completed her PhD on humpback whale behavio d is continuing with field research that takes her around the world. I ate about nature, wildlife and conservation, she writes about the sub he loves, including marine biology and the humpback whale. Ruth co s to being 'hooked' on studying and has almost completed a secor jree in Earth sciences, cosmology and particle physics, and she pla study philosophy next. Her triumphs and struggles to find and live own personal dreams provide the inspiration for much of her writing, iding *The Thinking Person's Guide to Happiness* and *Coping with Compu* *ating*, both published by Sheldon Press.

Overcoming Common Problems Series

Selected titles

A full list of titles is available from Sheldon Press,
36 Causton Street, London SW1P 4ST and on our website at
www.sheldonpress.co.uk

Body Language: What You Need to Know
David Cohen

The Chronic Pain Diet Book
Neville Shone

The Complete Carer's Guide
Bridget McCall

The Confidence Book
Gordon Lamont

Coping Successfully with Varicose Veins
Christine Craggs-Hinton

Coping with Age-related Memory Loss
Dr Tom Smith

Coping with Compulsive Eating
Ruth Searle

Coping with Diabetes in Childhood and Adolescence
Dr Philippa Kaye

Coping with Diverticulitis
Peter Cartwright

Coping with Family Stress
Dr Peter Cheevers

Coping with Hay Fever
Christine Craggs-Hinton

Coping with Hearing Loss
Christine Craggs-Hinton

Coping with Kidney Disease
Dr Tom Smith

Coping with Polycystic Ovary Syndrome
Christine Craggs-Hinton

Coping with Radiotherapy
Dr Terry Priestman

Coping with Tinnitus
Christine Craggs-Hinton

Depression: Healing Emotional Distress
Linda Hurcombe

Every Woman's Guide to Digestive Health
Jill Eckersley

The Fertility Handbook
Dr Philippa Kaye

Free Yourself from Depression
Colin and Margaret Sutherland

Helping Children Cope with Grief
Rosemary Wells

How to Be a Healthy Weight
Philippa Pigache

How to Get the Best from Your Doctor
Dr Tom Smith

The IBS Healing Plan
Theresa Cheung

Living with Birthmarks and Blemishes
Gordon Lamont

Living with Eczema
Jill Eckersley

Living with Schizophrenia
Dr Neel Burton and Dr Phil Davison

Living with a Seriously Ill Child
Dr Jan Aldridge

The Multiple Sclerosis Diet Book
Tessa Buckley

Overcoming Anorexia
Professor J. Hubert Lacey, Christine Craggs-Hinton and Kate Robinson

Overcoming Emotional Abuse
Susan Elliot-Wright

Overcoming Hurt
Dr Windy Dryden

Overcoming Insomnia
Susan Elliot-Wright

Overcoming Shyness and Social Anxiety
Ruth Searle

Reducing Your Risk of Cancer
Dr Terry Priestman

Stammering: Advice for all ages
Renée Byrne and Louise Wright

Stress-related Illness
Dr Tim Cantopher

Tranquillizers and Antidepressants: When to start them, how to stop
Professor Malcolm Lader

The Traveller's Good Health Guide
Dr Ted Lankester

Treating Arthritis – More Drug-Free Ways
Margaret Hills

Overcoming Common Problems

Overcoming Shyness and Social Anxiety

RUTH SEARLE

First published in Great Britain in 2008

Sheldon Press
36 Causton Street
London SW1P 4ST

British Library Cataloguing-in-Publication Data
A catalogue record for this book is available from the British Library

ISBN 978–1–84709–032–4

1 3 5 7 9 10 8 6 4 2

Typeset by Fakenham Photosetting Ltd, Fakenham, Norfolk
Printed in Great Britain by Ashford Colour Press

Produced on paper from sustainable forests

To my wonderful man, Dr Mike Butters ...
you make my life complete

Contents

Acknowledgements

My grateful thanks to Fiona Marshall for her help and support and to the editorial and production teams at Sheldon Press.

Introduction

Most human activities are social and we spend a lot of time interacting with, thinking about or being directly or indirectly influenced by other people. Our behaviour affects the way other people think, feel and act, and in turn their behaviour affects our own thoughts, feelings and actions. In fact, human interactions – our norms, conventions and institutions – structure the social groups and societies we live in.

At the very heart of social behaviour lies a person's ability to make sense of a social situation so that he knows what to expect and what to do. The interpretation of social behaviour varies from culture to culture and from group to group, as well as over time. In addition, our ability to interpret social situations involves a range of basic cognitive processes, including memory for people, places and events. This 'social cognition' depends on how we understand, perceive, interpret, store and respond to the social information that we receive.

We all form impressions of others – friends, neighbours, teachers, our family; in fact, virtually everyone we meet. We assign characteristics to them: for example, friendly, aggressive, helpful or selfish. This ability has evolved throughout history and has enabled humans to develop complex social groups. Group living is an intrinsic part of human nature and vital to our survival – our ancient ancestors had to contend with many dangers, not least the large predators that were around then, and living in groups bestowed many benefits. We are still social creatures today and although we don't meet too many predators on the high street (a debatable point!), we still enjoy the survival benefits of group living which have been responsible for the extraordinary success of our species.

As much of our behaviour is innate, we engage in a good deal of our social behaviour unconsciously and instinctively – that is, without our awareness. Our first impressions automatically activate stereotypes that have a lasting impact. This is part of our normal psychology – it helps us to 'read' other people, another crucial survival mechanism. However, when we observe someone else's behaviour we often make inaccurate and biased assumptions.

What's more, some people can become overly sensitive to and anxious about social interactions. This may be partly genetic, or it may be a learned behaviour. Whatever the cause, this heightened sense of self-awareness and 'other-awareness' can result in varying degrees of shyness or social anxiety. Shyness is seen in the vast majority of people at some stage in their lives, if only in adolescence. It is in effect an over-sensitivity in the normal psychological survival mechanisms that evolved to enable us to function successfully in groups. In other words, shyness is survival, of a rather over-sensitive kind. It may also have a biological cause and there is some evidence that an imbalance in the brain chemistry of people who are over-anxious in social situations may be to blame. We will look at all this in more detail in the first half of the book.

How this book can help

People who are socially anxious can have delightful personalities. They may have a great sense of fun, they may be kind, generous, sensitive, understanding and compassionate, and they may express all these facets of their character when they feel at ease. However, their true personality is often hidden from others and even from themselves because of their lack of self-confidence and poor self-esteem.

This book aims to show you that shyness is a natural part of being human – it may have evolved in humans as a necessary survival instinct. It explores how our personalities develop and how shyness may be a consequence of the way your brain is structured. (It also explains how you can rebalance your brain chemistry to help you feel more confident and improve self-esteem.)

We'll look at how shyness, rather than being a problem, can be seen as a gift and something that can be turned to your advantage. We will look at ways you can increase self-confidence and self-esteem, and discuss practical ways you can overcome shyness in certain situations. There will also be tips on meeting new people, having successful conversations and looking for a romantic partner.

I sincerely hope to show you that being shy can be something to enjoy rather than fear, and that it has many advantages both for you and the people who care about you.

Part 1

SHYNESS AND SOCIAL PSYCHOLOGY

1

What is shyness or social anxiety?

Shyness is a term that is widely used. Practically everyone knows what it means to experience shyness, or has felt shy at one time or another during their life. Even people who do not regard themselves as shy may also suffer from occasional social anxiety, for example when required to speak in public, or when meeting new people.

Social anxiety occurs when you believe that you might do something that will be humiliating or embarrassing in a social situation. It's when you think that other people are judging you in a negative light, and it makes you self-aware, self-conscious and afraid of being criticized, dismissed or rejected.

Shyness could be described as apprehension, anxiety and poor self-regard in social settings. People who are shy may experience problems in meeting people, making new friends, developing relationships with the opposite sex and enjoying new or different experiences. They may suffer excessive self-consciousness and lack assertiveness in expressing their opinions. Being shy can also lead to feelings of depression and loneliness.

Symptoms of social anxiety

The difference between normal occasional social anxiety and social phobia (the term given for the clinical diagnosis) is one of degree. While normal social anxiety can be distressing, it is more manageable than full-blown social phobia, which may cause significant distress and interference in a person's life. Whichever term is used – social anxiety, shyness or social phobia – the following symptoms will be common to all in varying degrees:

- worrying about what others think of you;
- worrying about what could go wrong;
- being painfully aware of what you say and do;

- having trouble concentrating and remembering what people say;
- having mind blocks and being unable to think straight;
- feeling nervous, anxious and self-conscious;
- feeling inferior;
- being frustrated and angry with yourself;
- feeling unhappy or hopeless about being shy;
- having problems expressing yourself: speaking too quickly, mumbling or gabbling;
- trying to melt into the background and avoid being seen;
- avoiding eye contact;
- avoiding difficult social situations or occasions;
- blushing;
- sweating or trembling;
- feeling panicky: breathless, pounding heart, feeling dizzy or sick;
- feeling tense and unable to relax.

You may be able to think of lots of other symptoms that you experience in difficult social settings. Some may give you more problems than others, but these feelings may cause you to avoid social situations, such as parties or even simply going out with friends. Shyness may be limited to certain aspects of your life, such as speaking in public, meeting new people you perceive as 'above you' or going on dates, or you may suffer from a more generalized social anxiety which affects many aspects of your daily life.

Perhaps you avoid situations in a very subtle way, without even being aware of it. Have you ever waited for someone you know to arrive before going into a room full of people? Have you hung around or helped in the kitchen at parties to avoid having to meet new people? Do you avoid talking about personal issues? Shy people avoid doing something because it causes anxiety.

You may also stick to situations where you feel safe. When you are with other people in social situations, it is difficult to predict what they will do. What if you are asked a question or introduced to somebody who makes you feel anxious (such as the boss)? What if someone asks for your opinion or asks you to do something, or even ignores you and talks to somebody else? What if you are left on your own with no one to talk to? All these things can cause anxiety in someone who is shy. They can lead to 'safety behaviours'. These behaviours include rehearsing what you will say to someone, hiding behind your hair or your clothes, sinking into the background, not talking about yourself, your opinions or your feelings, and staying with someone 'safe' such as a friend or in a 'safe place' such as the kitchen – while of course keeping an eye on an escape route, or preparing an excuse to leave early.

Shy people tend to dwell on the potential problems of a situation. All this worrying and apprehension spoils any social occasion before it's even begun. And if we do embarrass ourselves, shy people continually ruminate on what happened and relive the awful moment over and over again.

Shyness and social anxiety dent your self-esteem and your confidence and make you feel inferior to others. You begin to believe that everyone will reject you, ignore you or think you are inadequate. You may feel different from everyone else, and may be demoralized and frustrated.

Social anxiety and modern society

Because shyness and social anxiety are experienced in varying degrees, it is difficult to estimate the frequency with which they occur. However, recent estimates from researchers suggest that between 3 and 15 per cent of the population have the most severe form of social anxiety – social phobia – and it seems to affect men and women equally. The more usual forms of shyness and social anxiety are extremely common, and around 80 per cent of all people say that they experienced periods of severe shyness during childhood and adolescence. It seems that many simply 'grow out of it', since shyness drops to around 40 per cent of the adult population. Shyness and social anxiety appear to be widespread and are found in all cultures around the world. Only 5 per cent of adults say they have never been shy at all. You are certainly not alone!

In fact, it seems that social anxiety is on the increase. The reasons for this are not understood yet, but there are some interesting suggestions as to why it may be so. It has been thought that our automated society is reducing our contact and social interactions with other people. When you think about it, we do have far less direct communication with others than we used to just a few years ago. Instead of chatting to the person behind the counter at the bank, we get our money from an ATM or do our banking online; we send emails instead of having real conversations; many of our telephone calls are automated and we never get to speak to a real person; at work we spend much of our day interacting with our computer; and nowadays we can even meet friends and potential partners online rather than in real social situations.

No wonder people are becoming more and more anxious when having to interact with a real person! Children today spend more time in front of their computers and televisions than they do playing outside or interacting with other people. This could lead to an even bigger increase in social anxiety and social phobia in the future.

2

Evolutionary psychology

Evolutionary psychology studies the fascinating subject of how our behaviour has developed. Many animals are highly social. Their lives are centred on being with others of their kind. Humans are no exception and from our evolutionary beginnings we have been a social species.

Living in social groups has many survival benefits. Group living allows more effective food hunting, as well as better care of youngsters and defence of territory, but it also has costs. The more individuals there are living in a group, the more competition there is for resources such as food and mates, and for a space to call your own – whether it be a nest, a cave or a house. There is also an increased risk of infection.

Group living sometimes involves conflict. This is often resolved by a dominance arrangement, via either a single leader or a hierarchy of dominance – where there are 'layers' or grades of power or responsibility. In animal groups such as gorillas, a silverback male leads; wolves and dogs have a hierarchy of dominance or 'pecking order'. In human societies, too, we have many different hierarchies of dominance, from governments, institutions and companies to families and peer groups.

The success of a group requires cooperation, communication and group cohesion. Animals, including humans, must constantly make decisions about how to behave and act appropriately within a group – anything from which mate a female should choose to sire her offspring, to how to dress appropriately at a party. The more information you have about a situation, the better able you are to make a choice. Communication is a vital part of this.

Communication

In the natural world there is an astonishing diversity of species, each with its own communication signals, which have evolved over millions of years. Some animals, such as the blue whale, can communicate over whole ocean basins, while others need to be in close proximity or even physically touching. Some animals, such as chameleons, communicate by colour; some by chemical signals such as pheromones; some by rituals such as the dance of the honey bee. Groups also have their own sense of identity and develop their own defining 'signatures', such as uniforms or rituals. Humans have developed their own way of communicating via elaborate speech and non-verbal body language.

These signals enable animals to recognize members of their own group, and to understand subtle communications. The fascinating study of body language reveals the many signals we give out, most barely perceptible, but all sending messages about the way we feel. For example, if a person turns slightly away from you, folds her arms or avoids eye contact, you may get the message that she is not interested in what you are saying. If someone leans towards you with an open posture and lots of eye contact you feel encouraged to continue. These sorts of communication signals are vital, and help avoid conflicts between individuals and within groups such as families and communities.

Shyness as survival

The point is that you may be shy because of the way our ancestors evolved as social creatures. Humans probably inherited the primary emotions seen in all higher animals: fear/aversion, assertion/anger, happiness/satisfaction, sadness/disappointment. Recent research suggests that these primary emotions are hardwired into the older parts of the human brain. There is some evidence, however, that life in large communal groups was only possible because of the growing repertoire of emotional responses that developed in humans as they diverged from our primate ancestors.

Our ancestors had to develop the ability to cope with a range of social relationships through group solidarity, cooperation and tolerance. Conflict with other groups enabled them to create boundaries and maintain their own social groups more tightly, which also served as protection against predators. Fear and distrust of outsiders is widespread in both our nearest relatives, the chimpanzees, and in human groups (and could explain the incessant wars throughout human history). This natural xenophobia, coupled with the need to form cooperative, close-knit 'in-groups', resulted in the development of heightened emotional awareness – both self-awareness and other-awareness.

Imagine it … being part of a protective group was vital to every human being. To avoid being cast out, left at the mercy of the cold and the predators, it was crucial that you were accepted and valued as a member of your group. In all probability, if you were a little shy and careful about the way you behaved, you could avoid drawing too much attention to yourself; otherwise you risked being ousted from the group. It would pay you to be ultra-sensitive to the feelings and behaviour of other people. Looked at this way, shyness and social anxiety may have been vital for survival and an important part of our evolutionary psychology.

Early human groups

Let's take a brief look back at how social groups may have formed in human society to see how social anxiety and even social phobia may have developed.

It is now widely accepted that, around 7–4 million years ago, humans (hominids) shared a common ancestor with our closest relatives, the chimpanzees, bonobos (or pigmy chimps), orang-utans and gorillas (see Table 1, p. 12). Even after all this time evolving, we still share 97.5 per cent of our genes with chimpanzees. In fact we are more closely related to chimps than horses are to donkeys, dogs are to foxes or cats are to lions!

The oldest fossil remains of humans – *Australopithecus aferensis*, known as 'Lucy'– date from around 3.75 to 3.2 million years ago and were found in Africa. Lucy was still quite ape-like and ate a traditional primate diet, although she was bipedal (walked upright) like modern humans.

Little is known about the social behaviour of early humans but inferences can be made from our living primate ancestors, thanks to the pioneering work of researchers like Jane Goodall and Dian Fossey who studied primates in their natural wild habitat.

Social behaviour in primates

Chimps and bonobos are very social animals, friendly rather than aggressive. Disagreements and confrontations are generally settled without violence, and they usually live peacefully together. This is contrary to many earlier studies of captive primates, which reported their behaviour as innately aggressive and gave rise to the 'naked ape' theory of human aggressive behaviour.

Primate studies have also shown us that chimps, bonobos and gorillas quickly learn socially transmitted behaviour such as the use of tools. Chimps use stones to break nuts and use leaves for drinking, as well as sticks to collect termites to eat. They hunt small animals (which account for about 10 per cent of their diet) as an organized group. They share food, both meat and vegetation, and if an individual finds a new source of food, it will let the others in the group know.

A recent study has shown that chimpanzees are far more civilized than we give them credit for. They seem to be happy to help unrelated chimpanzees and unfamiliar humans, even if it means exerting themselves for no reward (one chimp helped an older arthritic chimp to climb a frame). This sort of behaviour – known as altruism – was thought to be unique to humans, but experiments in this study found that 12 out of 18 semi-wild chimps went out of their way to help. Bonobos also display altruism – one male bonobo even alerted zookeepers when an unrelated bonobo was drowning. These animals certainly seemed to be acting out of genuine concern for others rather than for a reward for themselves. More than can be said of some of our fellow humans on occasions!

Primates show elementary forms of communication using non-verbal gestures as well as a range of verbal sounds. Separate groups show a variety of different social behaviours, which indicates that it is not simply a matter of genetic programming but also a learning process. It is thought that primates, particularly the bonobos, display the same type of social behaviour that has traditionally been ascribed uniquely to humans. It may be that our early human ancestors of some 4 million years ago behaved socially just as primates do today and can provide us with insights into the social lives of our ancestors.

The first humans

The first indisputably human remains, dating from about 2.5 to 2 million years ago, were found in East Africa. These first humans were called *Homo habilis* or 'handy man' because their remains were found alongside stone tools. The brain case was much bigger than either Lucy's or the chimpanzees'. It is thought that the addition of more meat and omega-3 fatty acids (docosahexaenoic acid or DHA) in the diet allowed this extraordinary brain growth (DHA is the building block of brain tissue).

Around 1.8 to 1.6 million years ago, *Homo erectus* appeared in the human fossil record alongside a greater variety of stone tools (there may also have been wooden and bone tools which have not been preserved over time). Also called 'Java man', he had the largest brain yet of the human or primate lineage and used up to 25 per cent of his daily calorie intake to fuel this brain (monkeys use just 8 per cent). His diet included not only scavenged meat, killed by other animals, but meat from wild animals which he actively hunted himself. *H. erectus* was so successful that he outlived all other humanlike species on Earth at that time, surviving until around 300,000 years ago.

Homo sapiens or archaic humans evolved between 500,000 and 180,000 years ago. They gradually replaced *H. erectus* and lived alongside other early humans such as *Homo neanderthalensis*, or Neanderthals as they have become known. *H. sapiens* lived in social groups or communities and would bring food back to a home area, rather than roaming the countryside as their hunter-gatherer ancestors had done. They had mental maps of the best places to find food and hunt animals and had created special killing areas where they drove large prey over cliffs, so that they would fall to their deaths and provide huge amounts of meat for the whole community.

This required a great deal of cooperation and communication among the members of the group, and living in a group became absolutely vital for survival. You can imagine how it might pay to be quiet, unobtrusive and a little shy! It would also pay to develop a keen sensitivity to others in the group, to 'read' their feelings and be acutely aware of the impression you were making on others – the basis of social anxiety.

Early modern humans

As early humans began to share and barter for food and other provisions, they began to settle into a more sedentary lifestyle. Our own species, *Homo sapiens sapiens*, evolved some 40,000 years ago during the Stone Age or Neolithic period. They looked almost exactly as we do now, except they were leaner, fitter and taller. They continued

Table 1 A summary of human evolution

Years ago	Human evolution	Brain size (cubic centimetres)
7–4 million	Last common ancestor: human lineage branches off from chimpanzee lineage.	350
5 million	Bipedal – hominids begin to walk upright.	400
3.75–3.2 million	Lucy (*Australopithecus aferensis*). Still ape-like but bipedal. Hominids adapt to forest and grassland habitat, and combine hunting with foraging.	500
2.5–2 million	Early humans (*Homo habilis*) make sharp stone tools.	650
1.8–1.6 million	Java man (*Homo erectus*). Humans evolve less body hair and show changes in brain structure (possibly due to development of language), growing to over 1.52 m (5ft) tall.	800
500–180,000	Modern humans (*Homo sapiens*) evolve.	1000
40,000	Stone Age man (*Homo sapiens sapiens*). Population 5–10 million.	1400
12–10,000	First Agricultural Revolution. Farming begins with the domestication of plants and animals.	1400

to forage for vegetation, fruit and nuts, and to hunt wild animals for meat.

As the human population grew, Stone Age man began to grow food from seeds and to store it for the harsh winter. Around 12–10,000 years ago, hunter-gatherers became farmers and the first Agricultural Revolution occurred. Cereal grains were adopted as a staple diet and animals became domesticated. The advent of agriculture again demanded cooperation and successful group living. Farming was a cooperative activity, in terms not just of the farming work, but also of defending resources from outside groups. Being able to read your fellow humans was just as vital to survival as it had been in earlier times, but with the development of language and sophisticated tools, communication became much more complicated. Perhaps social anxiety actually increases as more demands are made on individuals to work as part of a team and fit in with the group. And now, with our complex modern systems of communication, this is truer than ever.

The development of social behaviour

There are two main sets of theories as to the development of human social behaviour and technological advancement. However, the arguments are still far from settled.

The first theory suggests that culture and language evolved around 2 million years ago during the time of *Homo habilis* and was due to humans having to cooperate in order to hunt and survive. In this theory the process of developing culture, language and human intelligence is seen as a long, cumulative evolution. The successive enlargement of the brain over the past 3–2 million years supports this idea and points to the development of cultural and social learning as a result of an increasing need for communication, cognitive skills and increasing dexterity for activities like tool making. Social interactions would have gradually become more complex over a long period of time.

The second theory suggests that our human ancestors remained relatively unchanged until a rapid acceleration in learning and cultural development occurred after the appearance of modern Stone Age humans, *Homo sapiens*, some 40,000 years ago.

The true story is likely to lie somewhere in between. Behaviour does not appear from nowhere; it is the culmination of prior learning. So it seems likely that there was a slow development over 2–3 million years ago around the time of *H. habilis*, followed by periods of rapid development when *H. sapiens* and *H. neanderthalensis* appeared, and again later during periods of change such as the advent of agriculture 10,000 years ago. Over the past 1,000 years there has been an explosive acceleration in the speed of technological advancement and this is likely to continue.

Increases in brain size developed as part and parcel of the increasingly complex repertoire of communication, language, greater sociability and manual dexterity for tool making. Survival began to depend on culture, social interactions and intelligence. Evolution would have selected these attributes, propelling humans toward ever greater social and cultural development. Perhaps shyness developed alongside these social and cultural changes in human societies, as part of sensitivity to those crucial social interactions.

Language

An increasingly complex language is a distinctly human feature that makes us unique, allowing us to describe abstract matters and refer to circumstances not actually present. Language enables us to separate the reality of the here and now from that of the past or future. We are able to access and discuss memories.

We also have an 'inner speech' that allows us to imagine new situations and create new goals. In other words, we can think in conceptual terms. We have developed the skill of reflection and self-awareness, which is a very human attribute. It is part of the complex consciousness that distinguishes us from most other species in the animal kingdom – but not all. Our closest relatives, the great apes, have also been found to have this highly evolved self-awareness, in experiments which test an animal's ability to recognize itself in a mirror. This is a definitive test of self-awareness where an animal is discreetly marked on its face, often the forehead. If it subsequently notices this mark in a mirror and touches the mark on itself, this is indicative of self-awareness. Human babies do not develop this trait until around two years of age.

Research has found that dolphins too have mirror self-recognition, and similar results are shown in experiments with elephants. It is easy to see how these animals possess such self-reflection and sensitivity when we consider the complex social groups in which they live. It is well documented that elephants appear to mourn their dead companions and seem to have specific elephant graveyards. This is surely a sign of social sophistication and complex consciousness.

As well as being aware of ourselves, humans at least are able to be aware of others. This other-awareness enables us to predict the feelings and motivations of others by reflecting our own feelings and motivations – this is known as attribution. We 'read' others by assessing the signals we receive from them on many different levels. Much of this communication, some suggest up to 80 per cent, is achieved by non-verbal means or body language – perhaps a relic of a means of communication our ancient ancestors used before the development of verbal language.

The features of language appear to be shared by most, if not all, languages. According to the psychologist Charles F. Hockett, there appear to be 13 separate features that are common to all languages. Our knowledge about language appears to be inborn, or innate or genetic, and to have developed because of our social interactions throughout the course of human evolution.

Children and language

Children are primed to learn language whether they are taught it or not. This, it seems, begins even before birth. Children the world over, whatever language they are brought up with, are self-taught linguists. As long as they are able to hear language, they will instinctively speak and learn the rules of language.

Human babies have an incredible ability to learn, and will learn more in the first two years of life than other species of animal learn in their whole lives. By 4 weeks, a baby can match his mother's voice to her face and by 12 weeks, he can identify her by sight alone. Babies not only recognize sounds but can remember the finer details of particular sounds such as stories or melodies. It is an evolutionary advantage for babies to bond with their mothers and so it makes sense to begin this process before birth. Experiments also show that babies prefer the language their mothers speak rather than a foreign language.

All children, regardless of their culture and language, seem to go through the same sequence of language development. At the age of one, a child can speak a few isolated words; at about two, a child can speak two- and three-word sentences; at three, sentences become more grammatical; and by the age of four, the child's speech sounds much like that of an adult. The fact that the sequence is so consistent across cultures indicates that human knowledge about language is innate and very rich.

In one study, researchers found that even deaf children of hearing parents began using a system of gestures called 'home sign' which eventually took on the properties of a language, even without any instruction in lip reading and vocalization. These children essentially created their own language and went through the same stages of development as normal hearing children.

Non-verbal communication

Non-verbal communication provides vital information about feelings and intentions. One study found that gesture plays an important part in understanding what people mean when they speak. In fact, people were almost twice as likely to understand the nature of a request when gesture and speech were used together as when speech alone was used. People who are shy can be overly sensitive to these gestures, sometimes misinterpreting their meaning, which leads to anxiety about what others really think of them.

Non-verbal cues are often reliable indicators of whether someone likes you. They can also be used to regulate interactions – for example to signal the approaching end of a conversation, or that someone else wishes to speak. Intimacy can be expressed by cues such as touching and mutual eye contact, and dominance or control can be established with non-verbal threats.

People tend to have less control over sending and receiving non-verbal communication than they have over speech, as non-verbal communication is often subconscious. Non-verbal sensitivity tends to improve with age, is more advanced among successful people, and is compromised among people with various psychological disorders. Women are generally more adept than men at detecting and sending non-verbal communication; however they differ less in their conscious awareness of exactly what information has been communicated.

Types of non-verbal communication

- **Eye contact** communicates a huge amount of information. People gaze more at others they like, and people of lower status gaze more at those of higher status than vice versa – except in situations where a person of higher status wants to exert control over one of lower status. While adults tend to gaze more when listening than when speaking, a speaker who increases her eye contact or 'gaze' signals indicates that she is about to stop speaking; a listener who reduces eye contact is indicating that she is about to start speaking.
- General **facial expressions** are a good indicator of a person's feelings. Research shows that facial expressions are universal indicators of the six basic emotions: happiness, surprise, sadness, fear, disgust and anger (although there are cultural differences in the expression of emotions).
- **The body** too is a means of non-verbal communication, with its postures and gestures. Posture can communicate liking. For example, people who like one another tend to lean forward, maintain a relaxed posture and face one another. It can also communicate status. Individuals of higher status adopt a relaxed, open posture, with arms and legs asymmetrically positioned and a backward lean to the body; conversely, those of lower status adopt a more rigid, closed and upright posture, with arms closer to the body and feet together.
- **Touching** means different things depending on the type of touch, the context within which the touch occurs, who touches whom, and what the relationship is between them. Touching can communicate things such as affection, playfulness, and control.
- The **amount of space** that people use to position themselves relative to others communicates intimacy and liking. There seem to be four interpersonal distance zones: intimate (up to 0.5 m), personal (0.5–1.25 m), social (1.25–4 m) and public (4–8 m).

People who are intimate stand close together while mere acquaintances stand further apart.

When you are shy or anxious, you can become acutely aware of every gesture and movement that others make. While this can be an advantage when trying to understand another person or sense an atmosphere in a room full of people, it can also become a burden and a source of misery.

3

How people think and feel about their world

When we attempt to understand people, we observe our own thoughts, feelings or actions. Generally, our intuitive attempts to apply reasoning and logic to our everyday life work very effectively. But we also make errors in reaching our social judgements. This leads to various psychological biases that may result in 'conditions' such as shyness and social anxiety – really, they are just variations of 'normal'.

Social schemas

Our thoughts, feelings, perceptions and beliefs about the world are organized in mental frameworks, or 'schemas' as psychologists call them. We have schemas for ourselves; for particular people, such as our best friend; for groups of people, such as nurses or solicitors; for events, such as how to order a meal in a restaurant; for roles, such as how waiters should behave; and also for places and objects. Schemas help us interpret the world around us. If you saw a policeman walking the beat in a pair of pink fluffy slippers, carrying a bunch of flowers, this would certainly not fit in with your schema about policemen!

We tend to acquire and develop our schemas through experience and exposure to the world around us: personal encounters, the media, stories told to us and so on. As we encounter more and more instances of a particular schema, it becomes more firmly embedded in our thinking.

Schemas of our social groups are particularly important because they characterize large numbers of different people into broad categories – for instance the British are known for their 'stiff upper lip'. Schemas of social groups are frequently described as stereotypes because they are often closely associated with prejudice, discrimination and inter-group relationships. Stereotypes are learned in early childhood through normal social training rather than direct experience, and exist to help people make sense of the world around them and bring meaning to their everyday experience.

Schemas of groups outside your own tend to be less favourable than those of your own group. And when someone is categorized as a member of a particular group, the schema, or stereotype, of that group influences the impression of that person. For example, if a student holds a schema of a university professor as being pompous and opinionated, then he will assume automatically that every university professor he meets will be pompous and opinionated, and that unfortunate prior impression will influence the entire interaction.

The concept of self

Our self-concept is based on schemas relating to the personal knowledge, ideas and feelings we have about ourselves. These are some of the most significant and influential frames of reference we have about the world. The self is a person's distinct individuality. The concept of self not only includes how we are, but how we would like to be, or how we ought to be.

So how do we learn about who we are and how do we form the schemas we have about ourselves? We learn partly from introspection and contemplating ourselves, but because of the extremely social nature of humankind, we learn much more about ourselves from how others treat us, and from how we think others view us. Research has shown that other people's expectations about us can in fact change the way we behave. For example, the psychologist Allan Snyder in 1984 reported a series of studies in which experimental participants behaved in a more extrovert manner simply because others were primed with a false expectation about how extroverted they were. These expectations actually made the participants behave in a more extrovert manner. There are other examples too, such as students who are expected to under-perform and whose grades actually fall because of this expectation (similarly, students who believe they are expected to do well often actually improve).

We often learn most about ourselves by simply observing how we behave. If we habitually behave in a certain way, we will come to believe that this is the sort of person we are. For example, if we sit quietly at home in the evenings and avoid parties and social events, we can come to believe that we are introverts. In turn, this fuels the expectations of others who reinforce our belief about ourselves.

Self-awareness

Generally, people are not consciously aware of themselves all the time. Self-awareness comes and goes for different reasons. Usually we just get on with our lives without particularly being aware of ourselves, but at other times we can be totally self-absorbed.

Self-awareness can have at least two different aspects: a private self – your private thoughts, feelings and attitudes; and a public self – how others see you, your public image. In this way, self-awareness can become apparent simply because you are in the presence of other people – for example, if you have to give a public talk or performance. Private self-awareness controls behaviour by matching your own internal standards, while public self-awareness controls behaviour by promoting the impression you make on others.

Social identity

Each of us, then, has a self-identity that is derived from our personal characteristics, such as having a sense of humour, and from our close personal relationships, such as family relationships, friendships and romantic relationships. We also have a social identity that we derive from the social groups to which we belong, such as gender, profession, age group and ethnicity.

Social identity is uniquely associated with group behaviour. By being part of a group, we categorize ourselves and others in the group in terms of our perceptions, attitudes, feelings and behaviour.

There is some evidence that people store information about the *individual self* and what is known as their *collective self* (self as a member of a group) in separate compartments. In other words, when people think of their personal qualities they are unlikely also to be thinking about their group membership, and vice versa. This means that either the individual or the collective self may have more importance. Some people are motivated more by their individual self-concept, others are motivated more by their membership of a group, which could be a romantic relationship, family or friends.

Self-esteem

People vary enormously in their level of self-esteem. It has been suggested that self-esteem is an internal indicator of social acceptance and belonging – a meter by which we measure ourselves and social situations. The idea is that the most basic human motive is to belong and to be properly socially connected (a concept that has important evolutionary connotations). Feeling good about yourself, or self-esteem, is extremely powerful indicator that one has succeeded in the pursuit of social connectedness. We will look at ways you can increase your self-esteem in Chapter 13.

Social inference

In order to make sense of the world, and to interact with people and get on in life, we need to have a basic understanding of how other people operate. We need to know why people do what they do if we are to be able to find our way through life in a way that enables us to make positive things happen for us while avoiding negative things. This is a skill that has evolved in humans as social animals, and it is seen in many other social species as well, including our closest primate relatives.

The most powerful knowledge we can have about people is causal knowledge. If we know what causes people to behave in certain ways then we are able to predict and influence what they will do. For example, most of us know that if we are nice to people they are likely to agree to do small favours for us, and that people who feel threatened or cornered can often lash out aggressively. This process allows people develop a commonsense causal understanding of human behaviour.

Predicting behaviour

When we try to decide the causes of behaviour in people, the most important thing we need to know is whether the behaviour is an accurate reflection of the person's disposition to behave in that way – whether it is normal behaviour for his or her type of personality – or whether it is a reflection of the situation he or she is in (people sometimes behave out of character in certain situations). One of the processes of socialization that we learn early in life is what behaviour we should expect in various situations. Once we learn that certain situations cause people to act in a specific way, we develop schemas for how we expect people to act in those situations. For example, when people are introduced to one another, they are expected to look at each other, smile and say something like 'Hello, how are you?' or 'It's nice to meet you' and perhaps shake the other person's hand. When people act in these conventional ways in certain situations, we are not surprised – their behaviour is apparently dictated by social custom.

As we get to know other people, we also get to know what to expect from them as individuals. We learn about their disposition – the kind of behaviour in which they tend to engage across all sorts of different situations. We learn to characterize people from a range of attributes such as being friendly, generous, positive, pessimistic, greedy or unhelpful, and we do this by observing their behaviour in a variety of situations. Sometimes we can even make decisions about people and inferences about their behaviour from a single observation. If someone's behaviour is very different from the way most people would act in a particular situation, we attribute their behaviour to internal or dispositional causes – we assume this behaviour is part of their personality. For example, if we see someone refuse to hold the door open for a person in a wheelchair, we attribute certain negative dispositional characteristics to them.

We also look at consistency – whether a person's behaviour occurs reliably in similar situations. For example, if you met a woman for the first time and she appeared to be very quiet and depressed, you might assume that she had a sad disposition. But imagine that a good friend of hers disagreed and said that she was normally very cheerful and happy; this new evidence about her behaviour might make you re-evaluate her and wonder if it was the situation that was causing her to be sad. This inconsistent behaviour leads you to seek external causes for it.

Finally, particular behaviours can be performed only in particular situations. Imagine for example that your work colleague was generally very pleasant and polite to everyone but was rather rude to one person in particular, every time she met him. You might conclude that this rude behaviour was due to some circumstances that triggered your colleague's behaviour and not to her normal disposition.

We engage in much of our social behaviour unconsciously, that is without our conscious awareness, and when we observe someone else's behaviour we make inaccurate and biased assumptions a great deal of the time. Our first impressions automatically activate stereotypes that have a lasting impact. Often, just being consciously aware of this natural and normal human tendency is enough to make us think about our behaviour and avoid making errors in our judgements.

Shyness and social anxiety

Human beings are unmistakably social creatures and a great deal of our life is spent in the company of others. Not only do we simply share our living space with other people, we psychologically associate in groups. A group is a collection of individuals who have developed a sense of who they are and how they should think, feel and behave – they generally have the same interests and goals. Being in a group can simply provide protection and allow people to do things they cannot do alone. However, there are much more fundamental reasons for people to belong to a group. Groups of people with similar attitudes and behaviours to your own provide a wonderfully comforting sense of self-validation. Groups can reduce anxiety, provide confirmation that your perceptions are correct and reduce uncertainty about your place in the world.

The need to belong to a group, whether it be the family, a peer group or the community, is one of the most fundamental of all human motivations. Simply being ignored or excluded from social interactions can have profound effects; indeed, many societies ostracize or exclude people as a form of punishment. Participants in experiments show signs of genuine distress – fidgeting, disengagement, displacement activities and so forth – when they are excluded from a simple and spontaneous game of passing a ball around a group of people.

The behaviour of other people has a powerful effect on our own behaviour. Studies have shown that the mere presence of others can affect a person's behaviour. One study showed that people performing a simple task such as turning the crank of a fishing reel performed the task faster and for longer if others were present. This happens because you become self-aware.

Social anxiety is the fear that you may do something that will be humiliating or embarrassing when exposed to the scrutiny of others. Because we are so dependent on that sense of belonging to a group, people who are anxious in social situations tend to expend a lot of energy and attention on worrying about how they are perceived by others present. Studies have shown that highly anxious individuals are better at detecting other people's negative behaviour, whereas individuals with low anxiety are better at detecting positive behaviour. People who are socially anxious tend to interpret non-threatening or ambiguous social events more negatively than other people.

Fearful shyness

Some psychologists believe there are two types of shyness: fearful shyness and self-conscious shyness. Fearful shyness starts early in life, often in the first year, and is sometimes called stranger anxiety. We will come back to this in Chapter 4, but generally, fearful shyness is the reaction of an infant to confrontation with unfamiliar people and includes wariness, retreat, and the seeking of security from the child's mother. Fearful shyness is not only seen in human infants but also among the young of most mammalian species. From an evolutionary perspective, this type of shyness makes sense because strangers may be associated with danger.

Fearful shyness usually decreases as children grow up and learn to cope with potential threats. However, in some individuals it persists as a form of social anxiety and results in people becoming upset about social interactions or experiencing fear when with others.

Self-conscious shyness

Self-conscious shyness occurs when people feel excessively exposed to the scrutiny of others and become acutely aware of themselves. This self-awareness in public results in embarrassment, awkwardness and blushing. Self-conscious shyness develops later on in childhood and in adulthood. It is part of the self-awareness we touched upon in Chapter 2 that is present both in humans and in our close primate relatives, and has recently been found in dolphins and elephants. The most important cause of self-conscious shyness is simply being conspicuous in public. Very few people like to be stared at since it makes them feel vulnerable – even perhaps that they are being criticized. Being conspicuous breaches a person's privacy – we become open to scrutiny by others. For example, teasing makes people become self-consciously shy, often to the extent of embarrassment.

In order to understand more about how shyness and social anxiety arise in individuals, we must look at how the personality develops throughout life, how it affects our perceptions of the world around us and how it influences our reactions and behaviour.

4

Social development

From before birth, through adolescence and into adulthood, each of us develops from a relatively unsophisticated bundle of reflexes into an amazingly efficient individual with well-developed language, perception and intelligence. As we grow, we rapidly acquire an impressive array of sensory, perceptual, social and cognitive abilities that define us as individuals.

Childhood

Because babies are totally dependent on their parents, the development of attachment between parent and infant is crucial to survival. Babies have the ability to shape and reinforce the behaviour of their parents and in turn, parents reinforce the baby's behaviour. This is the basis for the development of a solid attachment which provides a safe place from which babies can explore the new.

Attachment is seen in two forms of baby behaviour: stranger anxiety and separation anxiety. Stranger anxiety in babies between 6 and 12 months old consists of wariness and fearfulness, crying, and clinging to their carer when in the presence of strangers. Male strangers seem to generate the most anxiety, child strangers the least; women come somewhere in between. The response of the baby's carer (usually the mother) may dictate its response and do much to reduce anxiety – though an anxious carer will obviously increase the baby's anxiety.

Separation anxiety is a different set of fear responses such as crying, arousal and clinging to the carer, seen where the carer tries to leave the child. It first appears at around 6 months and usually peaks at about 15 months. There are three different patterns of attachment.

- *Secure attachment* is the ideal, when infants show a distinct preference for their mothers over a stranger, crying when their carer leaves but stopping as soon as she returns.

There are also two types of insecure attachment:

- *Resistant attachment* is seen when babies show tension when interacting with their carers. A baby may stay close to its mother prior to her leaving but show avoidance behaviour when she returns – it may cry or even push her away.
- *Avoidant attachment* is seen in babies who generally do not cry when left alone. When the mother returns, they are likely to avoid or ignore her. These children tend not to like cuddling.

In all these patterns, it is the mother's behaviour that appears to be the most important factor in establishing an attachment. The mothers of securely attached infants tend to respond promptly to crying and are skilled at responding to their needs. These babies seem to learn to trust their mother. Mothers who appear to be insensitive to their children's needs create avoidant attachment, while mothers who are impatient with their children's needs and uninterested in them tend to foster resistant attachment.

The pattern of attachment between babies and carers seems to be related to the child's social behaviour in later life. One study showed that children who were securely attached at 15 months were more popular and sociable with other children when they attended nursery at three and a half years of age. Insecurely attached babies, however, later experienced difficulties with social adjustments, had poor social skills and tended to be hostile, impulsive and withdrawn.

Attachment and the relationship between parents and children is also an important predictor of relationships between siblings. If both parents and carers (who are sometimes older siblings) are sensitive to the needs of all children in the family and not selectively sensitive to one, there is less conflict between siblings. Also, an inability in parents to control skirmishes and conflicts between siblings is associated with aggressive, antisocial behaviour (though bear in mind that some rough and tumble between siblings is entirely normal!).

Friendships with other children also form an important part of social development, particularly cooperation. As relationships develop with peers, children also show helping behaviour, whether or not it has been taught. A child may comfort another child who is crying, for example. However, the degree of helping behaviour can depend on whether children see others behaving in a generous and helpful way. Positive reinforcement will lead to development of this so-called prosocial behaviour.

Puberty and adolescence

The transitional stage between childhood and adulthood involves turbulent physical and social changes as hormones stimulate maturation of the reproductive system. People reach their ultimate height, develop increased muscle size and body hair and become capable of reproduction. In industrialized societies the average age at the onset of puberty has fallen from an average of between 14 and 15 years in 1900 to between 12 and 13 years today. This is due to improvements in childhood nutrition.

There is also a change in social roles. The dependency of childhood gives way to increased responsibility, and relationships with peers change. Sexual maturation has a profound effect on behaviour and self-concept, particularly sensitivity about appearance. Many girls worry about their weight, or the size of their breasts and hips, while many boys worry about their height, facial hair, the size of their genitals and their muscular development.

Most adolescents also display a form of egocentrism: self-consciousness. Some developmental psychologists believe that self-consciousness may result from the difficulty young people have in distinguishing their own self-perceptions from the views other people have of them.

Because individuals mature at different rates, adolescents find themselves more or less mature than their friends and peers. This appears to have social consequences, with early maturing boys more confident about themselves and their looks than late maturing boys. Early maturing girls, however, appear to show higher levels of unhappiness and concerns about their body (which can result in eating disorders) and show greater variability in their levels of self-esteem.

Adolescent boys and girls have different views of puberty. Boys look forward to increasing strength, freedom and social status, while girls become increasingly concerned over their appearance, body image, weight and shape – the beginning of the development of sexual identity.

The nature of friendships changes. Girls seek out confidantes rather than playmates, and boys join groups that provide mutual support as they assert their independence. Leisure activities also change. Early on, children might engage in social activities organized by adults, such as those based on groups or clubs (Brownies, Scouts, sports clubs, etc.). But as they progress through adolescence, children take more control over their leisure activities, experimenting with activities associated with adulthood such as drinking alcohol, smoking, taking drugs and sex.

Adolescence does bring conflicts between parents and children, but these are generally centred on relatively minor issues such as untidy bedrooms, loud music, clothes and household chores. Such difficulties are usually overcome and most adolescents hold the same values and attitudes concerning important issues as their parents do.

Adulthood

Generally, by the time people reach middle adulthood, they have made almost all of the major life decisions concerning marriage or cohabitation, having children, setting up a home or establishing a career. By about their late thirties to early forties, people feel at their most confident, most 'in control' of their lives and most productive, though some are more satisfied with their lives than others. Depression declines and women in particular feel they are better able to cope with life's difficulties than when they were younger. Adults, particularly women, report a heightened self-awareness and self-identity during middle age and often social anxiety and shyness diminish considerably. We can simply 'grow out' of shyness, it seems, at least to some extent.

There appears to be no scientific evidence to support the idea that people experience a mid-life crisis, as is commonly believed. However, Erik Erikson and Harry Levinson are two researchers who have proposed that adults encounter a series of crises that serve as turning points in their development, particularly in middle age, when goals and expectations are evaluated. Whether or not mid-life crises are a reality, people in middle adulthood do periodically contemplate or question the important issues in their lives and go through periods of reflection. Sometimes the results of this incur major life changes such as divorce or a change of career.

5

Personality

We are born with certain personality traits, often defined as enduring patterns of behaviour that are the result of the physical structure of our brain. In other words, our personality is part of our biological makeup. Although learning is involved and we are able to modify the characteristics of our personality, there is some evidence to show that our innate personality traits remain with us throughout life.

Numerous researchers have put forward hypotheses for describing and analysing personality traits and have come up with various ways of testing people to determine their personality type. A researcher called Raymond Cattell identified 16 personality traits that he believed were the foundations upon which personality is built, such as being submissive or dominant, shy or bold, tough-minded or tender-minded, trusting or suspicious, and group-orientated or self-sufficient. You can see that a person leaning towards certain of Cattell's personality traits would be inclined to be anxious or shy in social situations.

Another researcher, Hans Eysenck, identified just three important opposing factors in personality type: extroversion/introversion, neuroticism/emotional stability and psychoticism/self-control. Extroversion refers to a person with an outgoing nature; introversion refers to a person who prefers solitary activities. Neuroticism refers to someone full of anxiety, worry and guilt; emotional stability refers to someone relaxed and at peace with themselves. Psychoticism refers to aggression, egocentrism and an antisocial nature (as opposed to a term for mental illness, used by clinical psychologists); self-control refers to a kind and considerate nature and the ability to exercise control over one's behaviour. According to Eysenck, the most important aspect of a person's nature is determined by a combination of these factors. For example, someone who leans towards being stable and introverted might be passive, thoughtful, even-tempered, calm and reliable, while someone who is stable and extroverted might be sociable, outgoing, lively and chatty. While there are variations on both Cattell's and Eysenck's ideas, these basic classifications are supported widely in the field of psychology.

Another widely accepted model of personality types is Robert McCrae and Paul Costa's five factor model, which is based on an analysis of words used to describe people's behavioural traits. It includes extroversion, neuroticism, agreeableness, openness and conscientiousness. Within each of these five primary factors, the personality is determined by agreement or disagreement with statements and words which describe the personality, such as 'irritable', 'cheerful', 'productive', 'I really like most people I meet' or 'I have an active imagination'.

Can we inherit our personality?

Some psychologists, including Cattell and Eysenck, have shown that certain personality traits are likely to be inherited. Studies of twins can show whether a trait is inherited by comparing identical with fraternal (non-identical) twins, by comparing twins raised together with twins raised apart and by comparing biological with adoptive parents. Many studies have found that the personalities of identical twins are more similar to each other than those of fraternal twins, which indicates that these characteristics are inherited.

Some studies that compared the personality traits of identical twins raised together and those raised apart found no differences in personality between identical twins raised apart, even though they were significant differences in the family environment in which they were brought up. However, other studies, which compared the personality traits of parents with those of their adopted children, suggest that the family environment may account for some of the personality traits (around 7 per cent). This shows that heredity and environment interact together and that our personalities, while mostly inherited, are also affected by the environment we are brought up in.

But social interactions between an individual and family members also contribute to the shaping of personality. Because of inherited differences in personality, one child in the family may be more sociable, while another may be more introverted and solitary. These early social interactions may help to reinforce certain biological personality traits, or moderate certain behaviour. For example, if a quiet, introverted child is consistently encouraged to interact socially, it may lessen his or her tendency to be solitary.

Do we learn our behaviour?

Some psychologists are more interested in the ways in which a person's personality is affected by his or her environment and view character and its development as a process of social learning. This has led to various theories such as social learning theory, psychodynamic theory (such as that proposed by Sigmund Freud) and the humanistic approach.

Social learning theory

This emphasizes the relationship between our behaviour and its consequences: in other words, much of our personality is learned through interactions with our environment. A person may act because he expects to be rewarded or punished; for example, a little boy may learn that he can get something he wants from his little sister by hitting her. But on one occasion his parents catch him hitting her, they punish him for it and his behaviour begins to change. Learning is also achieved by observing the consequences that others experience as a result of their behaviour. For example, the little sister learns by observing her older brother that she too may be punished if she resorts to hitting people to get what she wants.

Some social learning theorists also believe that there is a locus of control, or subjective viewpoint, when a person either believes that she is responsible for her own behaviour (an internal locus of control) or that life is controlled by external forces (an external locus of control). People with an internal locus of control will work harder to obtain a goal if they believe that they can control the outcome in a specific situation, while people with an external locus of control tend not to try so hard and to blame others when things go wrong.

The psychodynamic theory

This takes the view that much of our behaviour is instinctive and subconscious and involves the struggle between our subconscious and conscious minds. The work of Sigmund Freud has had a profound and lasting effect on our ideas about psychology and the role of our subconscious in the development of our personality. Freud divided the mind into three parts: the id, the ego and the superego. The *id* is completely subconscious and contains the libido, which is the primary source of motivation and involves immediate gratification. For example, if you are hungry, the id compels you to eat; if you are angry, the id prompts you to strike out. The ego is the self and controls behaviour, acting as a mediator to the primary instincts of the id. The *ego* allows us to delay gratification until it is appropriate; for example, it might prevent you from hitting out at somebody if you feel anger. The *superego* is the conscience and determines which behaviours are allowed (the internalization of the rules and regulations of society), and uses feelings of guilt to punish wrongdoing and moderate behaviour. Freud believed the mind was full of conflicts between these three entities and that phenomena such as dreams, creative art and slips of the tongue (so-called Freudian slips) are some of the ways in which we show these conflicts working themselves out.

Freud's work (much of it considered sexist nowadays) has since been modified and developed by other psychologists, notably Carl Jung, Alfred Adler and Erik Erikson. Scientific research on personality has however largely discounted these ideas in the light of more rigorous research.

The humanistic approach

This emphasizes the positive, fulfilling elements of life and is interested in nurturing personal growth, life satisfaction and positive human values. It takes the stance that people are innately good and driven to reach their true intellectual and emotional potential (self-actualization). The two most influential humanistic psychologists, Abraham Maslow and Carl Rogers, both believed that people are motivated to grow psychologically and to aspire to higher levels of fulfilment, and that they are motivated by positive instincts.

Maslow believed that we must first satisfy our basic physiological needs for food, water, rest, security, love and friendships. Only then can we be motivated to develop the higher needs of our personalities, such as self-esteem, curiosity and a desire for harmony and beauty around us, as well as self-actualization and the achievement of our full potential.

Rogers believed that personality development is dependent on one's self-concept, and on the way one is treated by others. He argued that all people, particularly children, have a need for positive approval, love and respect from others and that the key to developing a healthy, balanced personality and a positive self-concept is through our relationship with others. Our feelings about ourselves are dependent to a large extent on what others think of us. Rogers called these criteria *conditions of worth*.

All these ideas about social learning have their supporters and their critics, but one of the main criticisms is that they do not account for the origins of personality. Many of these ideas describe the personality but they do not explain it. It is likely that both the genetic factors that determine the personality we are born with (based on the structure of our brain), and the environment and situations we find ourselves in, play important roles in shaping our personality.

Personality and the sexes

From an early age people of all cultures have believed that men and women are different physically and psychologically. They hold certain stereotypes, which in general are more flattering about men than women, even in these modern times. Men are stereotyped to be more competent, independent, decisive and logical whereas women are stereotyped to be less competent, competitive, ambitious, independent and active. However, thousands of psychological studies of sex differences have failed to confirm most of the stereotypes. The personalities of both males and females are actually more alike than they are different. For example, there are few significant differences between the sexes in terms of introversion and extroversion, intelligence or perceived career success.

But there are certain differences between the sexes in relation to social behaviour, particularly aggression. Males behave more aggressively than females in most cultures even from an early age. Females tend to be more sympathetic and expressive in their relationships with others than males.

Personality differences between the sexes are thought to have evolved in our ancestors as a result of the division of labour between males and females. Females required better interpersonal and nurturing skills while males needed to be efficient hunters and protectors of family and social units. Many of these differences are cultural, and they vary from culture to culture. Three different tribes in New Guinea show marked differences between the behaviour of men and that of women. Among the Arapesh tribe, both men and women are expected to be cooperative and sympathetic, just as we expect the ideal westerner to be. Among the Mundugumor, both men and women are expected to be fierce and aggressive like our western 'macho' man. Finally, among the Tchambuli the women shave their heads, are boisterous and provide the food, while the men tend to focus on art, their hairstyles and gossiping about women!

As society and living conditions change, so do the behaviour and personality traits of males and females. For example, the advent of the contraceptive pill and greater educational opportunities have given women more choice about when to start a family and how many children to have. Also, advances in technology have placed more emphasis on intellectual skills in the workplace than physical strength, giving increased opportunities for women.

Personality tests

When you get to know someone, you begin to understand something about their personality and the sort of person they are. You find out if they are outgoing, impulsive, thoughtful, moody, emotional, positive, shy, etc. because you have spent enough time with them to see their personality traits in a variety of different situations. Clearly, psychologists are not able to spend large amounts of time with people to learn about their personalities and so personality tests have been developed to try and measure certain personal characteristics. There are two main types of personality test: objective and projective tests.

- **Objective tests** usually contain multiple choice questions and true/false statements. The responses to the questions are contained within the design of the questionnaire. The questions asked are unambiguous and can be taken at face value. (The fun quiz below is based on objective personality tests.)
- **Projective tests** contain ambiguous items that are designed to tease out aspects of the participant's personality. They are designed by psychologists who believe that behaviour is determined more by unconscious processes than by conscious ones and that objective personality tests are too simple, although critics of projective tests suggest that they are not reliable indicators of personality. They include tests such as the 'inkblot test', in which people are asked to describe what they see in an ink blot. Their answers may reveal something about their state of mind, such as whether they are positive, happy, angry or depressed. There are other similar tests using pictures which participants are asked to describe or tell a story about.

There are many personality tests available and they are usually designed for a specific purpose – for example, to discover your leadership qualities or management potential in a work situation. Here's a fun quiz to see what your major personality traits are (don't take it too seriously). Circle the answer that fits you best, then count up the number of answers in each column.

Discover your personality traits

Part One
Which words describe you best? For each numbered pair choose one word from either column A or column B:

W	A	B
1	Quiet	Active
2	Anxious	Excitable
3	Reserved	Impulsive

W	A	B
4	Unsociable	Optimistic
5	Pessimistic	Changeable
6	Passive	Outgoing
7	Thoughtful	Sociable
8	Peaceful	Talkative
9	Reliable	Responsive
10	Calm	Carefree
11	Abstract	Practical
12	Assertive	Accommodating
13	Adventurous	Restrained
14	Realistic	Sensitive
15	Suspicious	Trusting

Answers: Part One
Mostly As: You are definitely introverted. You are a quiet, introspective type of person who is reserved and can be a bit distant unless you are with close friends and family. You enjoy your own company and keep your feelings under control, have fairly high standards of behaviour and are reliable. You are not aggressive and seldom lose your temper. You tend to plan ahead and not act impulsively. You are also organized and like a well-ordered life.

If you circled mostly A words between numbers 1 and 5, you also have a tendency to be anxious, melancholic and moody. You can be overly emotional. If you circled mostly A words between numbers 6 and 10, you are emotionally stable and have a practical, matter-of-fact outlook on life. If you circled mostly A words between numbers 11 and 15, you are also an intellectual thinker, assertive and can even be dominant with others. You are uninhibited and quite bold in social situations. You are self-reliant with a no-nonsense approach but can be jealous and suspicious of others at times.

Mostly Bs: You are definitely extroverted. You are sociable and enjoy parties. You have many friends and need people to talk to. You tend to dislike spending a lot of time alone. You crave excitement, can be impulsive and often take chances. You are generally carefree, optimistic and have a sense of fun, although you can be a bit aggressive and have a tendency to lose your temper on occasions. You can also be unreliable where others are concerned.

If you circled mostly B words between numbers 1 and 5, you also have a tendency to be touchy and sometimes a bit bad tempered. You can also be emotional and prone to depression. If you circled mostly B words between numbers 6 and 10, you are emotionally stable, even tempered and easygoing. If you circled mostly B words between numbers 11 and 15, you are a practical thinker and can be submissive and modest. You tend to be shy, restrained and inhibited but you are tender minded and gentle. You are trusting of others and very understanding.

Part Two

Which statement describes you best? For each statement choose one way to complete it from either column A or column B:

S		A	B
1	I tend to have ...	Lots of friends and acquaintances	A few close friends and acquaintances
2	I get my energy from ...	Being with other people	Being alone
3	At a party ...	I'm full of energy up to the end	I get tired toward the end of the night
4	I prefer ...	Going out with lots of other people	A quiet night at home
5	When meeting new people ...	I'm chatty from the very beginning	I tend to be quiet until I relax with them
6	I love meeting new people ...	Not usually. It makes me uncomfortable	Yes, I usually look forward to it
7	If I am asked to talk about myself, I ...	Feel awkward and embarrassed	Enjoy the conversation
8	At an interview, I am ...	Nervous and have trouble remembering what to say	Fairly relaxed and focused
9	If someone asks me a personal question, I ...	Blush and feel self-conscious	Give them a cheeky answer
10	If asked to volunteer to do something difficult, I ...	Stay quiet, in case I'm not good enough to do the job properly	Volunteer – I'm as capable as anyone else of doing a good job

Answers: Part Two: Statements 1 to 5
Mostly As: You are an extrovert! You enjoy parties and social gatherings and look forward to meeting new people. You gain energy from being around others and interacting with them and you can party all night. You are focused outward, very sociable and outgoing. You probably have lots of friends and acquaintances and love chatting about anything and everything. In relationships, you tend to want to talk about things and get them out in the open quickly.

Mostly Bs: You are an introvert! You tend to prefer to be quietly at home, reading, thinking or studying. You feel uncomfortable and nervous meeting new people and tend to feel tired and drained when you are around others for too long. You gain energy from being quiet and alone. You are focused inward and probably have a few close friends. You tend to prefer small gatherings where you can enjoy good conversation rather than lots of social chatter. In relationships, you tend to think things over and talk about them when you are ready.

Answers: Part Two: Statements 6 to 10
Mostly As: You are shy! You tend to worry about what others think of you and avoid being put on the spot. You need time to think about what you say and do. You tend to worry about what could go wrong and sometimes feel inferior to other people. When in company, you tend to be a bit scatty at times and have trouble remembering what you were going to say, even though you are perfectly focused and have no trouble when you are alone. If you have to meet new people, you generally feel nervous and self-conscious and tend to be quiet until you settle down and feel a bit more comfortable with them. When you do speak, you sometimes have trouble expressing yourself. Maybe you gabble to hide your nervousness or you speak too quietly or too fast. If you can, you tend to hide away in the background and let others take the limelight.

Mostly Bs: You are not shy! You believe you are as capable as anyone else and are not afraid to have a go at new things, even if you do feel a bit nervous at first. You can be impulsive at times and if things go wrong, it doesn't worry you too much – after all, we are only human ... You are usually relaxed and focused on the conversation when you are with other people. You have pretty good concentration and know what you want to say. If you have to meet new people, you look forward to it and get chatting straight away. You find it interesting to discover what others think. When you speak, you feel confident and have no trouble expressing yourself. In fact you can be the life and soul of the party.

Shyness and introversion/extroversion

Extroverts tend to be outgoing and sociable, have lots of friends and gain their energy from being with other people. Introverts, on the other hand, prefer to stay at home quietly and tend to have just a few close and long-term friends. They gain their energy from being alone. You may think that because you are shy, you are also an introvert, but this is not necessarily true. You can be shy and extroverted. If in Part Two of the test above, you answered mostly Bs for statements 1 to 5 but mostly As for statements 6 to 10 then you are a shy introvert. If you answered mostly As for statements 1 to 5 but Bs for statements 6 to 10, then you are an introvert but not necessarily shy. You may simply be introverted and prefer your own company rather than to be with other people.

Traditionally, people have lumped shyness and introversion together. It makes sense, as both shy and introverted people tend to be quiet and prefer their own company to large get-togethers and noisy parties. They tend to be reserved, private people who prefer to stay away from the demands and stresses of the world. Indeed, researchers have found that there is a modest connection between shyness and sociability; shy people do tend to be less sociable. But a significant number of people who are shy are still very sociable; in other words they are shy but extroverted. Research has shown that sociability, in other words extroversion/introversion, and shyness should generally be considered to be separate concepts.

Shyness is an ultra-sensitivity that causes an emotional response – self-consciousness and self-protection. Introversion on the other hand is related to energy – the extrovert gains energy from social interaction, while the introvert gains energy from within (this may also be related to brain structure, as discussed in Chapter 6).

Carl Jung worked on introversion/extroversion and in his view neither type was superior; they were just different. Each has certain advantages. Extroverts gain an advantage from their outwardly focused personality as it allows them to nurture social contacts and work with others as part of a team. Introverts gain an advantage from their inward focus by contemplating the world around them on a deeper level.

Introverts, with their probing minds, are more likely to appreciate the complexities of life and be innovative and independent in their thinking. Academics and intellectuals tend to be introverts. Introverts have always been seen as 'different' and comprise less than 25 per cent of the population. Extroverts have traditionally made up around 75 per cent. However, today's modern lifestyle, with the influence of computers and the internet, has increased the number of introverts in the population to around 45 per cent and decreased the number of extroverts to 55 per cent. This trend is set to continue.

The shy introvert

This is the most challenging position. You may actually be introverted because of your shyness, with anxiety and concern over social interactions causing you to withdraw from people. You may be quite happy to be at home if you are a true introvert, but if you are only introverted *because* of your shyness, it can become a handicap leading to unhappiness, loneliness and depression. You may have become more and more isolated because you have few friends and social contacts to connect you to the outside world. You may have withdrawn more and more into a lonely life that you don't actually want, but your fear and anxiety of reaching out to others for social contact keeps you a prisoner of your own inner world. You will need to use all the tools in this book to help you overcome your shyness and make the social connections you need in your life. Later in the book you will find lots of tips to help you in this quest.

The non-shy introvert

These social types are the most misunderstood. As a non-shy introvert you have a quiet, reflective nature, spending much of your time alone, absorbed in your own work, interests and hobbies. You probably enjoy reading, writing and contemplating the world. You are focused inward and most people would probably think you are also shy. However, when you are in social situations you have no problems interacting with other people, chatting, meeting new people and behaving like an extrovert. You probably look forward to the occasional social get-together and can be perfectly sociable when you want to be. This is confusing for other people, but as we have seen, shyness and introversion/extroversion are separate concepts. As a non-shy introvert you tend to invest your psychological energy very carefully in the right places and with the right people. The more introverted you are, the less energy and patience you have for small talk, gossip or social chitchat. You tend to enjoy conversations more when you feel the content is meaningful. People seem to get 'mixed messages' from you; one day you are the life and soul of the party, the next you need space to be alone. This social style of yours can cause misunderstandings with others – you need to explain this to important people in your life. Overall, you are probably perfectly happy with your social style.

Many famous people have been introverts, including Abraham Lincoln, Albert Einstein, Alfred Hitchcock, Thomas Edison, Grace Kelly, Gwyneth Paltrow, Bill Gates, Clint Eastwood, Steve Martin, Harrison Ford and Michelle Pfeiffer.

Albert Einstein was known for his love of solitude. Dennis Brian's biography *Einstein: A Life* tells how as a child Einstein was actually thought to be mentally disabled or 'dull witted' because he was so quiet and withdrawn. He was described as a nervous, withdrawn dreamer. Luckily, following a move from a repressive school environment in Germany to schools in Italy and then Switzerland he became more outgoing and humorous, even though he remained an introvert. Introverts who are in the public eye are often driven by their quest for meaningful work or because of extraordinary circumstances rather than for the sake of fame itself. Like any other introvert, they need to recuperate with time spent in quiet contemplation.

The shy extrovert

These social types are in a better position than the shy introvert since they are more likely to get out into the world and interact in social situations. If you are a shy extrovert you will be overly sensitive and self-conscious in social situations but you will love being with other people nonetheless. While you might be anxious or feel threatened in the beginning, once you relax and muster your courage to get involved, you can be the life and soul of the party. You may need a few tips here and there to help you overcome your anxiety and self-consciousness in social situations, but generally your outgoing nature will ensure that you get out, meet people and enjoy the social side of life. On the other hand, your shyness may be so debilitating that you find it excruciatingly painful to interact socially. In this case, being a shy extrovert may be even worse than being a shy introvert because being with other people is so important to you. Introverts are naturally more content to be alone.

The non-shy extrovert

These social types have no problems meeting and interacting with other people. As a non-shy extrovert, you are likely to be outgoing, have lots of friends and acquaintances and gain your energy from social occasions. If you are a non-shy extrovert, you may find it difficult to understand social anxiety or indeed introversion, but hopefully this book will give you some insights into your shy or introverted friends.

We will come back to introversion and shyness in Part Two of this book to discover how people who are shy or introverted are misunderstood by others and what can be done about it.

6

Personality and the brain

Mechanisms in the brain are undoubtedly involved with personality traits; brain damage can produce permanent changes in personality and drugs that affect particular neurotransmitters in the brain can alter people's moods and anxiety levels. Advances in our understanding of the brain have been made after several decades of experimental research, culminating in modern neuroimaging methods such as functional Magnetic Resonance Imaging (fMRI), which can study the structure of the living brain, and Positron Emission Tomography (PET) scans, which measure brain activity.

One researcher, Edward Zuckerman, believes that extroversion is caused by sensitivity in the brain's neural circuitry that responds to reinforcement, punishment and arousal. He suggests that the brain mechanisms of extroverts are particularly sensitive to reinforcement and that extroverts participate more in social activities in order to receive more of this reinforcement. Neurotic personality types are sensitive to punishment and are anxious and fearful. The neural systems responsible for this response appear to involve the amygdala (a region of the brain involved in emotional responses). People with psychotic personality types are sensitive to arousal/excitement but have a low sensitivity to punishment. They have difficulty learning when *not* to do something.

Hans Eysenck also believes in the biological nature of personality, with introverts experiencing relatively high levels of cortical excitation and activity, while extroverts have relatively low levels. In order to maintain the optimum arousal level in the cerebral cortex, an extrovert needs more external stimulation than an introvert. The extrovert seeks stimulation from external sources by interacting with others in social situations or by pursuing new and stimulating experiences. Introverts avoid external stimulation to maintain their cortical arousal at an optimal level.

Shyness and brain structure

Other studies have investigated whether there is a brain mechanism responsible for shyness. One study showed that about 10 to 15 per cent of children between the ages of two and three become quiet, watchful and subdued when they encounter an unfamiliar situation. In other words, they are shy and cautious when presented with new stimuli. Shy children show signs of inhibition, such as clinging to their mothers or staying close to them, remaining silent and avoiding strangers or other novel stimuli. Children who are not shy do not show these inhibitions; they approach strangers and explore new environments.

The physiological responses of the children were also measured, and marked differences were found between the shy group and the non-shy group. Shy children were more likely to show an increase in heart rate, dilated pupils and raised levels of stress hormones than the non-shy group. The shy children obviously found the situation stressful, whereas the non-shy children did not. The results suggested that shyness may be caused by the excitability of the neural circuits in the brain that control avoidance behaviours. The investigators in this study also found that shyness was an enduring trait over the seven years that the study lasted, suggesting that we are born with shyness as part of our personality.

The amygdala and hippocampus

The amygdala and the hippocampus are deep-seated structures in the brain, which have been well studied in relation to fear and anxiety. There is substantial evidence to show that the amygdala is involved in fear and anxiety, both in animals and humans, and is responsible for certain emotional responses. Experiments with neuroimaging have shown activity in the amygdala when subjects are presented with anxiety- or fear-provoking stimuli. When the mechanisms involving the amygdala are oversensitive, people experience heightened fear and anxiety.

The hippocampus has a role in memory and cognition and is also involved in emotional responses such as fear and anxiety. An ancient part of the brain involved in the fight or flight response, the hippocampus evolved in our ancestors over millions of years.

Excessive activity in certain mechanisms within the hippocampus results in fear and anxiety – even memories of anxious experiences can stimulate both the hippocampus and the amygdala to produce feelings of fear and anxiety. Neuroimaging studies, using PET scans, of patients with anxiety or panic disorders have shown an increase in glucose metabolism in the left part of the hippocampus when compared to the scans of people without such disorders. In other words, the hippocampus is more active in people who suffer with anxiety – another line of evidence to suggest that social anxiety is part of our natural personality.

Both the amygdala and the hippocampus are connected in the brain and work together. They work as an ancient alarm system and are a primitive part of our brain, designed to warn us of threats in the environment such as predators or competing tribes. When this system is over-sensitive it produces an emotional overreaction, which results in general feelings of fear and anxiety and is thought to be the neurobiological cause of shyness and social anxiety.

Serotonin

In addition to over-activity in these brain structures, it is thought that imbalances in a neurotransmitter called serotonin can also produce anxiety and social phobia. Although it is unlikely that just one neurotransmitter alone is responsible, there is substantial evidence that serotonin plays a key role in the control of anxiety. The types of neurons that use serotonin in the central nervous system are particularly dense in the amygdala and hippocampus. However, the specific functions of serotonin and its relationship to social anxiety need further study, and drug treatments designed to increase serotonin have had mixed results. It has been suggested that these treatments may desensitize the fear circuits in the brain and when used alongside psychological therapies, such as Cognitive Behavioural Therapy (CBT), could reduce social anxiety in stressful situations. Some of these treatments have increased sociability in healthy volunteers as well as those with social anxiety. However, not enough is known about the role of the serotonin system in social anxiety, and indeed even in social phobia, to say with any certainty that treatment with drugs would be successful.

Stabilizing brain chemistry

Despite the uncertainties of the exact role of serotonin in social anxiety, it is widely accepted that serotonin significantly affects our mood and mental state, creating a sense of relaxation. Levels of beta-endorphin and blood sugar also control brain chemistry and consequently affect how you feel and act.

As well as creating a mellow feeling of being at peace with the world, serotonin also influences self-control, impulsive behaviour and the ability to plan ahead. Low levels of serotonin can create depression, lack of concentration, anxiety, impulsive behaviour and cravings for alcohol, sweets or carbohydrates like bread, pasta and cereal.

Beta-endorphin is a powerful chemical responsible for the so-called 'runner's high' or 'endorphin rush' and a sense of euphoria and well-being. The emotional effects of beta-endorphin can radically change the way you feel. When beta-endorphin levels are low, you may feel depressed, hopeless, isolated, emotionally overwhelmed and tearful. You will probably also suffer from low self-esteem. Since endorphins are our body's natural painkillers, low levels of beta-endorphin can lower your tolerance to pain considerably. Interestingly, you may also crave sugar. Sugar is known to increase levels of endorphins, which is why we love chocolate! Glucose is used as an analgesic for babies undergoing painful procedures in hospital, since it helps release endorphins. Dr Elliot Blass discovered this through experiments he carried out in the mid 1980s.

Glucose is a very simple sugar obtained from the digestion of carbohydrates. It is a basic fuel of all the cells in your body, particularly the brain cells that require a constant supply in order to function. When your body has the optimum blood glucose level, you feel great, but when blood glucose is too low you suffer the symptoms of hypoglycaemia. These include constant fatigue, restlessness, confusion, poor memory and concentration, and irritability. In diabetics, hypoglycaemia can be a very serious condition requiring hospitalization.

Normally, the body balances serotonin, beta-endorphin and blood glucose so that brain chemistry remains at optimal levels.

However, because of the heightened sensitivity of the brain circuitry within the mechanisms responsible for introversion and extroversion (the amygdala and the hippocampus), imbalances can have significant effects on your emotional feelings and behaviour.

It is almost impossible to isolate which of these biochemicals may be responsible for the symptoms described above; one or all could be out of balance. However, by tackling all three, together with simple lifestyle and dietary changes, it is possible to rebalance your brain chemistry to optimize serotonin and beta-endorphin levels and to stabilize blood glucose. Balancing all three of these biochemicals is not only crucial for your general health and well-being, but could help to reduce your social anxiety and increase feelings of self-esteem and the ability to cope in stressful situations.

So how do you balance brain chemistry?

First, because both low levels of serotonin and low levels of beta-endorphin create cravings for simple carbohydrates (sugars) such as bread, pasta, cereals, cakes, biscuits, sweets and chocolate, blood glucose levels can become erratic. You are likely to experience sudden increases in blood glucose followed by sharp dips that result in the symptoms of hypoglycaemia (including fatigue and feeling shaky or irritable). This is because simple carbohydrates are digested easily, broken down rapidly into glucose and released into your bloodstream too quickly. More complex carbohydrates such as whole grains, baked potatoes and green vegetables take longer to digest and release glucose more steadily into the bloodstream, avoiding these sudden increases and decreases in blood glucose. It is actually very dangerous for your body to have high levels of blood glucose and so there are several mechanisms designed to maintain the optimal level of glucose in the blood. One mechanism is the release of the hormone insulin, which transports glucose out of the blood and into the cells to be burned as fuel.

The problem is that our bodies are not designed to cope with simple carbohydrates and processed foods, so as blood glucose rapidly increases, your body overreacts and releases more insulin than is needed. This results in too much glucose being transported into the cells followed by a sharp drop in blood glucose, in other words hypoglycaemia. To compensate for this your liver will release glucose (this amazing organ stores about 400 calories worth of glucose as an energy backup) to keep vital organs such as your brain functioning properly. When this supply is used up, you start craving sugar again and the damaging cycle of high blood glucose followed by hypoglycaemia is perpetuated.

The surge of glucose in the blood can also cause adrenal fatigue. Every time your blood sugar spikes rapidly, your adrenal glands release adrenalin – the hormone that gives you a quick charge of energy. This response evolved in our ancestors and is responsible for the fight or flight response – just what you need to escape from danger, but detrimental to your body when this reaction is triggered several times a day. This vicious circle of hypoglycaemia and adrenal fatigue is bound to have a significant effect on your brain chemistry and consequently on the way you feel and act. It may also contribute to your feelings of anxiety in social situations.

More about serotonin and beta-endorphin

However, this is not the full story. While instability in blood glucose levels, sugar sensitivity and hypoglycaemia are well documented in their relation to our emotions, information about serotonin and beta-endorphins is not widely available to the general public. Yet both these biochemicals have significant effects on your physical and emotional health. Imbalances cause dramatic variations in your emotional outlook, your levels of anxiety and your ability to cope in stressful situations.

Both serotonin and beta-endorphin are neurotransmitters with their own unique molecular shape. Each carries its own distinct message via your neurons, or brain cells. Because of its unique molecular shape, each neurotransmitter requires a unique neuro-receptor, which sits on the surface of the neuron and only accepts messages from its own neurotransmitter. A molecule of serotonin can only transmit its message to a serotonin receptor – likewise with beta-endorphin transmitters and receptors. This permits communication between neurons in the brain and happens very rapidly. For example, if you were to hit your thumb with a hammer, you would immediately feel intense pain, but within a short time your thumb would become numb and you would begin to feel clear, focused, relaxed and a little 'spaced out'. These feelings are caused by the release of beta-endorphin molecules, which are the body's natural painkillers. In fact they are just as effective as morphine!

When levels of serotonin or beta-endorphin are low, there are fewer molecules available to attach to the neuroreceptors on the surface of your brain cells. So, in order to mop up the few molecules that are available, the brain creates more neuroreceptors. This process is called *upregulation* and is a mechanism designed to balance your brain chemistry.

It also works the other way round. If you have too much serotonin or endorphin, your brain becomes overloaded and it will shut down some of its neuroreceptors so that fewer molecules can attach to the neuron. This process is called *downregulation*. Downregulation is the same mechanism that causes people to develop a tolerance to a drug. For example, molecules of the painkiller morphine are shaped like beta-endorphin molecules and will fit the beta-endorphin neuroreceptors. When you take a morphine-like drug your brain senses an overload and begins to close down some of the neuroreceptors – in other words, it downregulates. The result of this is that you need bigger and bigger doses of morphine to control your pain.

The same thing happens with serotonin. People taking drugs like Prozac, which mimic serotonin, need bigger and bigger doses to have an effect on depression because of downregulation.

Sugar and brain chemistry

Beta-endorphin is an endogenous opioid, which means that it is found naturally in the body. Like other opioids the correct levels of beta-endorphin not only control pain, they also produce a sense of well-being, emotional stability and increased self-esteem. In addition they relieve some types of depression and control anxiety, paranoid feelings and anger.

Now, here's where the sugar comes into it. Sugar causes the release of beta-endorphins (so does alcohol). In normal brain chemistry, this has a moderate effect because there are a moderate number of neuroreceptors for beta-endorphin. However, if your beta-endorphin levels are naturally low, your brain, through upregulation, will have created more neuroreceptors and the sudden rush of sugar-induced beta-endorphins will create a heightened beta-endorphin response. Elliot Blass, who conducted experiments on the pain-relieving effects of sugar, found through his experiments that sugar blocked emotional pain just as effectively as it blocked physical pain. No wonder we seek out ice cream, chocolate, bread and pasta to make us feel better. It's like being high on opiates!

The problem with all this is that while people with normal body chemistry experience this beta-endorphin effect as simply a pleasant feeling, people with sensitive brain chemistries experience a feeling of euphoria that is powerful enough to create a drug-like craving for sugar or alcohol. Much of the time, low levels of beta-endorphin create feelings of loneliness, isolation, anxiety, depression and low self-esteem and it takes a 'sugar high' to feel better. Effectively, if your beta-endorphin level is naturally low, you may be living with anxiety and low self-esteem that is caused by your biochemistry. This will not be relieved by counselling or psychotherapy and not, in the long term, by constantly craving and eating refined sugar. The sugar-induced feelings of happiness and high self-esteem are short-lived and create a destructive vicious circle.

There is a similar scenario for serotonin. When you have naturally low levels of serotonin, it can make you feel depressed, unfocused and prone to impulsive behaviour. Your brain does everything it can to increase the levels of serotonin by the mechanism of upregulation and the creation of cravings for sugar that are used to make more serotonin.

Serotonin is made from the chemical tryptophan, an amino acid produced from the breakdown of protein. When you digest protein foods such as meat, fish and nuts, tryptophan is transported into your bloodstream. However, in order to make serotonin, tryptophan has to get into your brain and it can only do this by being transported alongside carbohydrates (carbohydrates are broken down into glucose – the fuel of the brain). This is why chocolate makes you feel good – it helps to raise serotonin levels when there is enough tryptophan in your bloodstream. However, the downside of relying on chocolate to raise your serotonin levels is obvious. Not only do you risk putting on weight but you also perpetuate the problem of sugar spikes and dips, which result in hypoglycaemia.

Drugs for serotonin

Some people suggest that the best way to raise serotonin levels is to take antidepressants such as Prozac, since most work by increasing the number of serotonin molecules available for neuroreceptors. They effectively achieve this by recycling used serotonin molecules and getting more use out of the serotonin you have. These drugs do work – but at a price. Just like the chocolate 'treatment', there are problems associated with taking antidepressants. There are some unpleasant side-effects such as reduced libido, nausea, jitteriness, sleep disturbance and strange dreams, but the main problem is that, because of downregulation, you will need more and more of the drug over time in order to have the same effect. You cannot stay on antidepressants for ever, and when you come off them you are still faced with the problem of naturally low serotonin levels. At best antidepressants are a temporary solution to severe depression – they are not suitable for the long-term management of low serotonin levels.

Happily, there is a wonderfully simple and natural solution. By making slight changes to your eating habits you can stabilize your brain chemistry, optimize glucose availability and beta-endorphin levels and get tryptophan into your brain to produce the correct levels of serotonin.

Natural remedies to stabilize your brain chemistry

The following are some of the ways in which you can change your eating habits and rebalance your brain chemistry:

- Reduce or better still cut out simple carbohydrates and processed foods such as sugar, sweets, cakes, pastries, bread and most cereals.
- Eat more complex carbohydrates and low glycaemic index (GI) foods such as green vegetables, fruit, whole grains, oatmeal and bran.
- Eat three meals a day or several small meals throughout the day to help stabilize blood glucose.
- Eat protein at every meal to produce optimum levels of tryptophan in your bloodstream.

- Eat a carbohydrate snack such as a baked potato in the evening to facilitate the transport of tryptophan into the brain in order to produce serotonin.

By stabilizing blood glucose and avoiding sugar spikes and dips throughout the day, you will stabilize beta-endorphin levels. By eating protein at every meal, you will build up your tryptophan levels throughout the day to ensure that there is sufficient to be transported into the brain to produce serotonin. There is a lot of competition from all the other cells in your body for amino acids, which are used for building and repairing tissue. There may not be enough to produce sufficient serotonin and this is why you should eat enough protein at every meal. By eating a carbohydrate such as a baked potato before bed, you will make sure that tryptophan can be carried into the brain to make serotonin as you sleep.

As your brain chemistry begins to stabilize, the downregulation and upregulation mechanism will also settle into a normal moderate pattern and you will avoid creating a destructive vicious circle.

These simple measures can help to make you feel more energetic, focused, emotionally stable and confident. They may also help ensure that anxiety in social situations is not caused merely by an imbalance in brain chemistry. It is well worth making some simple changes to your diet, which could make profound improvements to your emotional well-being. It won't happen overnight, but give these changes at least six months and monitor how you feel. It's a good idea to keep a journal or diary of both your diet and your feelings over this time.

Part 2

OVERCOMING SHYNESS AND SOCIAL ANXIETY

7

The problem with being shy

Although introversion/extroversion and shyness are considered to be different concepts in the scientific community, they are still usually confused by the world at large. Whether you are just shy, shy and extrovert or just an introvert, it is worth considering how these social types are seen by others, and what can be done to correct false impressions.

It seems that people who are shy or introverted are frequently misunderstood. They are often accused of being self-centred and unsociable, and it is easy to see why when introverts prefer to shut themselves away from the rest of the world. However, far from being selfish, introverts are frequently the opposite. Their inward focus and reflection allows them to understand the external world and the world of other human beings far better. People who are introverted or shy tend to have the capacity for extraordinary empathy, thanks to their ability to be perceptive, intuitive, and sensitive to other people's feelings. Introverts are not antisocial; they are just social in a different way. Introverts enjoy meaningful social connections and intimacy, but they need and prefer to have a few close relationships rather than lots of friends and acquaintances.

While extroverts gain energy from social interactions, introverts use enormous amounts of energy in order to engage with others, and so they spend that energy very carefully. They prefer meaningful conversations rather than general chit-chat and prefer small groups of close friends to large or impersonal social occasions. Introverts tend to speak when they have something to say rather than for the sake of talking, and this is frequently misconstrued as being withdrawn or antisocial.

Because introverts have traditionally made up the minority of people in the population, extroversion is seen as 'normal' and this influences the general concept of sociability. Because the majority of people tend to lump introversion and shyness together, those who are shy – whether or not they are introverts – can be misunderstood and classed as unfriendly or self-centred. For someone who is shy, this is a devastating accusation and could not be further from the truth. Shy people may withdraw even further into their shell because they are misunderstood in an extrovert world. So what can cause these misunderstandings?

Differences in social styles

The gap in understanding between the extrovert world at large and a person who is shy or introverted comes about through fundamental differences in their social styles. Introverts think and behave differently. Introverts may not be consistent in their behaviour from day to day because of ebbs and flows in the energy they have available for interacting with others. People who are shy can also show inconsistencies in their 'shy behaviour', since their levels of anxiety will vary according to the social situations they are faced with and the people they are with. Some circumstances cause more anxiety than others and all these factors can cause confusion and misunderstanding in people who are naturally extroverted.

For example, imagine you sit next to a man sitting alone on a park bench. You say a cheery 'good morning' but he glares back at you, with barely a nod in acknowledgement. You immediately feel unsettled. What is he thinking? Would he rather be alone? Has he just had bad news? Are you annoying him? Is he unable to speak? You would not know if this person felt angry with you for sitting next to him, whether he was preoccupied with problems of his own, or whether he was just nervous and shy. All sorts of things would go through your mind, and yet if that person had turned to you and engaged in conversation, you would know exactly where you stood with him. Being socially withdrawn in an extrovert world, which expects everyone to be sociable and chatty, does cause confusion and perhaps suspicion in people with no insight into these different social styles. Here are some examples of the way both introverts and shy people can cause confusion because of their behaviour:

- They can be absorbed in thought or paralysed by fear.
- They hesitate before speaking and may appear to lack confidence.
- They hate crowds and prefer to be alone.

- They are choosy about the social activities they will engage in.
- They are not forthcoming with their ideas or opinions.
- They are reflective and cautious.
- They become irritated when they do not have enough space to be alone.
- They are agitated by too much noise.
- They are difficult to read by their gestures and facial expressions.
- They are quiet and it can be difficult for others to get to know them.
- They may appear to be deliberately hiding something because they don't speak up spontaneously.

People who are extrovert and not shy may have difficulty in understanding these behaviours. It's all too easy for them to accuse someone of being aloof, sullen or antisocial when she is in fact either anxious and distressed because of her shyness or has a completely different social style because she is introverted.

Breaking the ice

Just realizing how you might come across to other people can help you to overcome your shyness long enough to break the ice in social situations. People who are shy or introverted are acutely sensitive to others' feelings, and this quality can be used to overcome that primary inertia you may feel when meeting somebody new or when you arrive at a social get-together. Try to step 'outside yourself' and look at your behaviour in the way that other people do – realize that while you are floundering around trying to think of something to say or frozen with nerves, other people may think you are being difficult or aloof. This is the last thing you want, of course, and the best way to deal with any awkwardness is to let people know that you are having difficulties. We all understand the feeling of nervousness and it is actually quite endearing to find someone who is a little nervous. By showing that you are nervous and that you need a little time to relax into a social situation, you will get people on your side, rather than letting them believe that you are simply self-centred or ignorant and falling into a downward spiral of negative feelings and reactions. So how can you achieve this?

When you meet other people, there is a lot you can do to break the ice:

- **Smile.** Even a small nervous smile can speak volumes. A smile will immediately disarm people of suspicion or negative opinions. It will instantly show that you are not actually sullen, depressed or antisocial but that you are friendly and open to social contact. A smile will also help you to feel more relaxed and positive. If someone smiles back at you, which they usually will, those good feelings will be reinforced and your confidence and self-esteem will crank up several notches. Smiling is a fantastic way to break the ice and show you have good intentions, and better still is a genuine big smile and a warm 'hello'. If you can manage this, it sets the tone from the beginning and people will see you in a positive rather than a negative light. It's a good start ...

- **Adjust your body language.** An open body posture will also present you in a positive light. People who are sullen, unfriendly and unapproachable adopt a hunched or closed-in position with arms and legs crossed and head held low. They avoid eye contact. When *you* meet people, make sure you face them, sit or stand straight, uncross your arms and legs, hold your head up, smile and maintain eye contact. If someone is speaking to you, respond by looking at them and answering or nodding in the appropriate places. If you can manage to remember these simple rules and try to relax when you meet somebody, you will immediately disarm them of their suspicions that you are difficult or antisocial.

- **Show interest in the other person.** One way to take the focus away from your own self-consciousness is to take an interest in the people you are with. Find out something about them beforehand, if possible, and ask them to tell you about their work and their interests. While they are talking, take some deep breaths and relax. Keep your mind on the person who is speaking. Before you know it, you will be thoroughly engaged in social interactions and the worst of your nervousness about meeting people will be over.

- **Have some control over the conversation.** Part of being shy is worrying about what people think of you, about saying the wrong thing or that your mind will go blank and you will have nothing to say. One way to overcome this is to have a degree of control over the conversation. Have some conversation starters up your sleeve, such as topical news items or stories that might be of interest to the group of people you are with. The internet is a great place to start and you could even make some notes to refer to if your mind goes blank. It's a good way to make sure that you have something to contribute and prevents people from seeing you as awkward or uninterested.

- **Change your focus.** It's difficult to get over your feelings of anxiety and self-consciousness 'from the inside'. It's like not being able to see the wood for the trees when you are embroiled in your own feelings. Try to change your perspective and 'get outside' yourself. Be an observer on the outside watching your behaviour and try to see how you come across to others – see yourself from the outside. This is called dissociation and we will come back to this in Chapter 12. It can take some getting used to, but it is a worthwhile exercise and will enable you to see yourself as others see you. If this is difficult for you, try to imagine that you are watching somebody else who behaves the same way as you do. Imagine you are your own best friend – what advice would you offer to make sure you are not giving people the wrong impression?

Shyness and feelings of guilt

Throughout childhood, adolescence and often into adulthood, the behaviour of people who are shy or introverted is constantly compared with the more widespread social style of extroversion. They are accused of being 'dreamers', being too slow or too quiet and, of course, being antisocial. Most shy or introverted children and young adults wish they could 'join in' more or be more 'normal'. They grow up feeling inferior and believing there is something wrong with them because they are not extroverts. In adulthood, many intelligent and successful introverts still believe they have major defects and feel guilt and shame for the way they are. This is simply a reflection of the ignorance and prejudice in our culture as a whole. We have all learned that extroversion is the way we *should* be. In fact it is not the *only*, or indeed the *best* way to be.

Because of this skewed judgement, people who are shy or introverted often feel disproportionate feelings of guilt, which can cause them to withdraw even further. Because they are so sensitive to social atmospheres and to other people's feelings (and are usually acutely observant), they worry about the effect they have on other people. For example, someone who is shy or introverted will worry about 'bothering' others; he will avoid interrupting them or asking for help in case he is making a nuisance of himself. People who are shy or introverted worry unnecessarily about mistreating others and doing or saying the wrong thing. They are oversensitive to other people's feelings or needs. It is important to take a reality check, or you will end up feeling depressed and miserable, forever trying to please everyone else:

- Ask yourself whether you *really did* hurt someone's feelings.
- Remember that you are oversensitive and re-evaluate the situation.
- Try to ask if you have hurt someone's feelings – more often than not it will just be your imagination.
- If you really have hurt someone's feelings in some way, then simply apologize and move on. We are all human beings and we all make mistakes from time to time. Forgive yourself and stop dwelling on it. Learn from the experience but put it behind you and get on with your day – there is nothing to be gained by going over and over what went wrong.

Remember you will never be able to please everyone, and while you are worrying about the effect you have on other people you are not being true to yourself.

8
Shyness is a gift

As we have seen, there are inherent problems with being shy or introverted and having to deal with other people in social situations. Shyness is often considered a handicap or a psychological defect which has to be eradicated. People who are shy or anxious are advised to come out of their shell, take social risks and get over their shyness as if it was an abnormality that was intolerable. But let's look at it another way for a moment. Being shy could actually be a huge advantage. Your shy personality has many attractive, positive and desirable traits; qualities that are often lacking in the vast majority of people. Shy people tend to be:

- romantic
- sensitive
- reflective
- conscientious
- compassionate
- responsive
- caring
- thoughtful
- loyal
- contemplative
- quietly spoken
- gentle
- considerate
- empathetic
- warm
- giving
- understanding
- good listeners
- faithful
- patient

- lifelong friends
- easygoing
- reliable
- modest
- dignified
- well-mannered
- calm.

Now what is so bad about that? These are wonderful and desirable qualities to have as part of your personality. Yet they are not appreciated because society promotes an aggressive, extroverted, talkative and outgoing social style as the only approach where anyone can achieve success and happiness in life. This is clearly not true.

Just think of all the remarkable people in the world who are quietly getting on with their job of caring for others, often for little or no financial reward. Frequently they are engaged in work that is demanding, difficult and sometimes emotionally heartrending: nurses, doctors, aid workers, emergency workers, volunteers, carers, conservationists – the list goes on and on. Many of these people could be classed as shy, quiet or introverted and they usually do their work with little fuss, far away from the limelight. They may be motivated more by their compassionate nature and sensitivity to the needs of others than by financial reward, or the desire for recognition. There are, of course, many people who are not shy or introverted who are engaged in meaningful, compassionate work. But the point here is that many unsung heroes, making marvellous contributions to the world, are dismissed and overlooked because of their quiet, unassuming, shy characters. Shyness should be considered a gift.

Qualities of shyness

Let's look more closely at a few of the qualities that being shy brings to the world.

Sensitivity

Sensitivity is the ability to respond to people on a deep emotional level and to care for and about others with extraordinary empathy. Shy people are often extremely sensitive and can be hurt very easily by brash, critical people or harsh environments. However, this does not mean that people who are shy and sensitive cannot have a high degree of self-esteem and self-confidence.

Sensitive people are able to understand and empathize with people who are sick, discriminated against, rejected or abused and those who are troubled, lonely and isolated. Sensitive and shy people are able to identify with others and understand life from somebody else's perspective. Because of this they tend to be extremely conscientious and hate letting other people down; this makes them solid and reliable friends, partners and work colleagues. They also tend to be more faithful in romantic relationships and form enduring, often lifelong, friendships. Embrace and celebrate the sensitive side of your personality!

Modesty

Most shy people are also very modest. They quietly go about their business, working hard, helping others and even making extraordinary contributions to society without seeking continual praise and recognition. Their sense of self-worth comes from giving to others in a quiet, graceful, sincere and dignified way – it is not based on what others think of their contribution.

Modest people are sometimes thought of as being 'too nice' or as something of a pushover, but this is not necessarily true. People who are shy and modest often have great inner strength, self-respect and wisdom. They usually know when others are abusing their good nature or failing to show them respect and can be tough-minded when required. When someone who is modest feels that she is being taken for granted or exploited, she is likely to pull away in a quiet and dignified manner rather than explode in an angry outburst. Modesty and humility should never be mistaken for weakness.

Thoughtfulness

Shy people and introverts are usually deep thinkers. They are intelligent, thoughtful and reflective and far from being 'self-absorbed' or 'selfish' they live in a different kind of world. They think and analyse the world around them and make commitments and important decisions only after very careful consideration.

Being a good listener

Everybody loves a good listener and yet people who really listen are very hard to find. Shy people tend to talk less than average and be extremely good at listening to others. Researchers found that the more a person talked, the less he or she seemed to listen. Those who talked more than average, that is more than 25 per cent of the time, did not appear to understand their partners in conversation as well as the people who listened more and talked less. The people who listened not only paid attention to the actual words being spoken but also showed considerable skill at detecting the emotional nuances of a conversation. In other words, shy people tend to be sensitive listeners who are able to pick up the emotional meaning of a message as well as the actual words that are spoken.

This is a skill that is in big demand in our modern, fast-living society where everyone wants to be heard. Being a good listener is a wonderful attribute that can help establish rapport and deepen relationships with others.

Kindness

Shy people are generally gentle, sensitive souls who are kind to others, slow to anger and respectful. In this harsh world where wars, violence, terrorism, cruelty and aggression seem to be on the increase, we need more kind-natured people to bring us hope and renew our faith in humanity. Shy people dislike conflict and violence and long for peace in the world. We need an antidote to the aggressive, domineering, disrespectful people in this world who all too often get what they want only because they shout the loudest.

Research has shown that people who are shy, particularly women, will go out of their way to please others and tend to behave in a non-threatening, friendly and polite way. Shy people can still possess inner strength and stand up for what they believe in – gentleness and kindness should never be misunderstood for weakness. People who are shy and sensitive to the needs of others will often treat others with respect, gentleness and kindness because that is how they would like to be treated themselves. They go out of their way to avoid hurting anyone and have a rare insight into the human condition that allows them to understand on a deep level how other people might feel. This wonderful quality makes a shy person very special and desirable.

Loyalty

Social interactions and forming relationships can be difficult, yet shy people can make the most true and loyal friends and the most loving and faithful partners. They think deeply about their relationships and make commitments very carefully, so once they find the right person they will invest a great deal of time and energy in making a relationship work over the long term.

Research has shown that in romantic relationships, shy people tend to be more monogamous and faithful than people who are not shy. Shy people are more likely to be selective in their choice of partner and get to know him or her well before making a serious commitment. This approach is more conducive to successful and long-term relationships. Shy people tend to stay for the long haul and are prepared to work hard at a relationship. The partners of shy people tend to see them more positively than the partners of non-shy people and describe them as sincere, dignified, calm, patient, sensitive and modest.

Shy and introverted people tend to take relationships more seriously and have fewer friends and acquaintances than those who are not shy. They tend to label people as friends only when they have a close relationship, and they value these friendships and will work hard at overcoming difficulties. This is refreshing in a society where marriage breakups are on the increase and people are too busy to nurture meaningful relationships with others.

What are your qualities?

Do you appreciate and embrace all the wonderful qualities you have in your shy personality? Probably not. You probably hear and remember the negative or critical things people say about you but rarely remember the compliments. Now it's time to redress the balance!

In the table on the next page write down all the positive qualities you believe you have – don't be modest! I've put in a few words and phrases to get you going ...

sensitive	intelligent	a good listener	modest
loyal	kind	trustworthy	empathetic
a good friend			

Keep this list and refer to it often! Add to it whenever you think of something else or when someone pays you a compliment.

9

Coping with social anxiety

I hope now you accept that shyness constitutes a perfectly normal social type. You are not unusual and shyness is not a defect; in fact it is increasing in society as a whole. Hopefully you also embrace and welcome certain aspects of your shy personality such as sensitivity, empathy, being a good listener, being a good friend and all the other wonderful attributes of being shy.

But, despite all these positive aspects of being shy, you may still be struggling with feelings of self-consciousness, embarrassment, anxiety and stress in social situations. There is no easy answer, but in this section I outline some techniques (most based on Cognitive Behavioural Therapy) that you might find helpful.

What do you want to change?

You may feel at times that you just want to change everything – to stop being self-conscious, embarrassed, feeling nervous, etc. In other words, stop being 'you' and start being confident and charismatic in any social situation.

Obviously that's a tall order for anyone, but, more importantly, you shouldn't force yourself to change – not least because trying to change your basic personality will simply result in unnatural and forced behaviour. If you are naturally introverted or shy and sensitive in social situations, you may never become the life and soul of the party. That's fine; why not leave it to someone else? What's more important is your social comfort. It is far better to learn to accept, embrace or nurture the aspects of your personality that are difficult or impossible to change and concentrate your efforts on changing the aspects that *are* amenable to change. First you have to decipher which is which.

There are four main areas of your body and mind that are affected by shyness and social anxiety: your body, your feelings, your thinking and your behaviour. The following are some signs and symptoms you might experience in each of these areas:

Body

- dizziness/fainting
- pounding heart
- breathlessness
- tension
- sweating
- trembling
- blushing

Feelings

- panic
- nervousness
- fear
- self-consciousness
- apprehension
- anger
- frustration
- inferiority
- depression
- hopelessness
- sadness
- loneliness

Thinking

- acute self-awareness
- worrying about what others think about you
- worrying about what could go wrong
- forgetting what you want to say
- difficulty in concentrating
- mind going blank
- scatty thinking
- dwelling on things after the event

Behaviour

- avoiding eye contact

- melting into the background
- speaking quietly or finding it difficult to speak
- trying to stay 'safe' by staying in 'safe places', talking to 'safe people' and having 'safe conversations'
- avoiding certain social situations
- spending time alone when you'd rather be with other people.

All these aspects work together, often in vicious circles, and the combination of the way you think and behave and your self-consciousness and poor confidence interferes with you being yourself and showing your true personality in social situations.

Let's start by defining what you want to change. Think about how your social anxiety affects your life, about the signs and symptoms you find most distressing and about which aspects you want to change the most. To get you thinking, fill in your answers to the following questions:

How does shyness and social anxiety affect you?
Which aspects bother you the most?
What would you like to change?

It might help to keep a journal or diary of your feelings, especially in relation to your social interactions with others. Sometimes our feelings become a tangled, self-conscious muddle. Keeping a journal can help you to disentangle the various aspects of your shyness and identify individual signs and symptoms.

Please remember that everyone, whether or not they are shy, can be awkward in social situations. It is perfectly normal sometimes to say the wrong thing, interrupt in the wrong place, talk for too long, not talk at all, tell bad jokes, unwittingly offend someone, forget people's names or forget to thank the host ... the list goes on! Most people accept these social blunders as perfectly normal and the people who make them are still loved, admired and respected. It is better to be spontaneous and be yourself than to be constantly worrying about social conventions – and don't forget we all have 'bad hair days'!

Making a start

Keep your journal for a while and spend some time thinking about the ways that shyness affects your life and the things you want to change the most. For example, you may be longing for some romance in your life but are too shy to get out and about to meet new people. One solution could be to start with internet dating (more about this in Chapter 14) or attend that office party you've always avoided up to now. Make a list of all the aspects you want to change and brainstorm some possible solutions, even if they feel a bit too adventurous at the moment.

Keeping perspective

Anxiety can tend to dominate your life and it is easy to let things get out of proportion. If you dwell on your problems, you can end up feeling like an emotional wreck. One way to get some perspective on your problems is to make sure that you get involved with all sorts of things you enjoy doing, whether or not they entail meeting other people.

You can still enjoy being solitary and it is important and healthy for everyone to spend time alone. Being alone is not the same thing as being lonely but if you *are* feeling a bit isolated and cut off from others, at least you can fill your time with interesting, challenging or creative activities until you build new social networks.

Make a list of all the things you enjoy doing on your own. Remember the things you used to enjoy doing and think of all the new things you'd like to try. Here's a list to get you thinking:

- take a regular walk in the country or along the beach;
- get a dog;
- become a volunteer dog-walker at the rescue kennels;
- redesign your garden or help an elderly neighbour with his/her garden;
- buy a skipping rope or an exercise DVD, or take up yoga;
- make your own wine;
- grow your own vegetables;
- learn to play a musical instrument;
- help someone who is disabled;
- try out some new recipes;
- paint a landscape;
- draw a series of wild animals;
- write a short story or a novel;
- redesign a room in your home;
- read a new book;
- get a kitten;
- explore new places – hop on a train and visit a new town;
- plan a holiday or expedition;

... and lots, lots more.

You may even be able to develop some of your new hobbies into 'low-pressure' social activities – a great way to meet people who are on the same wavelength as you. For example, if you start walking in the country, you could join the local ramblers' group and enjoy walking with other people. By walking dogs at the rescue kennels, you could find yourself becoming more involved with voluntary work there and meeting other people who love dogs. You could begin writing a novel and end up joining the local writers' circle. You could redesign a room in your home, discover a passion for interior design and end up with a new career. You could even visit a new town and meet the love of your life!

The main thing is to keep a sense of proportion about your problems. Don't let them interfere with your enjoyment of life. You may find that you become more comfortable with other people and focus less on your own self-consciousness when you have lots of interesting things to talk about and share.

10

Change your thinking

In order to make lasting changes to your life and overcome some of the problems associated with being shy, you need an overwhelming desire to change, along with the belief that it is possible. Sometimes this happens when we reach absolute rock bottom and are so unhappy with our circumstances that we will do *anything* to improve them. I sincerely hope you have not reached this point, but it is important that you really *want* to change and *believe* that you can change in order to overcome your problems. Clearly you want to change since you are reading this book, but what about belief?

Belief

There are two kinds of belief: belief in yourself as a worthwhile human being and belief in your ability to achieve success. First, you *are* a worthwhile human being and you have many wonderful qualities to offer. You have as much right to be here as anybody or anything else – in fact the world *needs* you. With all the arrogance, anger, violence, intimidation and downright disrespect in this modern world, we need your gentle, sensitive, reflective and compassionate nature to redress the balance. There are not enough shy people in the world! Remember that shyness is a gift.

Look at the list of positive qualities you created earlier, believe in yourself as a worthwhile human being and don't try to change your basic personality type. You may always have a tendency to be a little shy and sensitive in social situations, but the aim is to reduce your anxiety and change your beliefs sufficiently that you feel comfortable interacting with other people, so that social anxiety no longer interferes with your life.

Second, you need belief in your ability to succeed. We are conditioned throughout our lives to believe other people's opinions of us. Usually we get a fair mix of positive and negative conditioning, but if we are adversely affected by negative conditioning, it can take some soul searching and hard work to reach a new way of thinking.

However, within every adversity lies opportunity. As we are a reflection of what we get from the world, it can work the other way too. If you believe with real feeling that you are confident, genuinely interested in other people and have real self-esteem, then behave accordingly ... the world will reflect that back to you. For the world to change and treat you differently, *you* have to change.

People don't like change and our subconscious minds will always resist it, so we become entrenched in our conditioned beliefs. The good news is that you can change the way you behave without even having to believe it at first. If you act in a confident manner, people will reflect that back and begin to regard you as a confident person. That in turn will increase your confidence and so on. You can 'fake it' until it becomes real if that's what it takes to change the way you interact with the world around you.

Faulty thinking

There are several ways that our patterns of thinking cause problems and distortions which prevent us from making real progress in our quest to change unhealthy behaviour. Before a troublesome social event, we often make predictions about what could go wrong and about how our faults will be put on show for others to see; during the event, we may try to guess what other people are thinking and inevitably assume that they think badly of us, even when they do not; after the event we dwell on the things we think went wrong and criticize ourselves undeservedly. These faulty thinking patterns can be very destructive but are very common in people with social anxiety.

Here are some other ways we distort the truth with faulty thinking:

- We take things personally and assume that people's words and actions are directed at us – 'he only left the room because I arrived'.

- We try to guess what people are thinking and assume they are judging or criticizing us – 'she thinks I'm stupid'.
- We take the blame, even when it is not our fault – 'I should never have said that'.
- We reject positive things that people say about us because they couldn't possibly be true – 'he's only saying that to make me feel better'.
- We believe that if something does go wrong it will be a catastrophe – 'if I make a mess of this, she'll *never* speak to me again'.
- We over-generalize and believe that if something bad happens once, it will always happen that way – 'I'll never be able to get the joke'.
- We jump to conclusions – 'they are bound to think I'm too quiet'.
- We use derogatory names for ourselves and put ourselves down – 'I'm stupid … useless' etc.
- We engage in wishful thinking – 'if only I were more intelligent/ attractive/confident …'

The only way to correct faulty thinking is to challenge your beliefs and the ways you think about yourself. Pretend you're having a discussion with someone who is totally opposed to your point of view – be the Devil's advocate! If necessary, get someone else to help you with this and ask them to challenge your beliefs.

There are many ways of thinking about things, and getting into negative or faulty patterns of thinking can prevent you from making changes that are necessary. For example, if you were told that you were 'different', you could either believe that you were different in a positive way (it's good to stand out from the crowd) or you could believe that someone was criticizing you (because they think you are abnormal).

The way we choose to think about things is just that – our choice. Because we are shy, our thoughts are biased towards supporting our beliefs about being inferior, but we can choose to correct that bias by challenging and questioning our beliefs.

Challenging your beliefs

Try to seek an alternative viewpoint and get into the habit of asking yourself questions designed to challenge your beliefs. It is worth writing down your answers to help you demolish your faulty patterns of thinking and focus on more constructive alternatives. Consider the following:

Imagine you are at an important social occasion. You are feeling nervous as you enter the room, and are about to try and melt into the background and hide behind your drink when you spot the host dragging a rather stern-looking man over to meet you. You immediately begin to panic as you realize there's no way out of this. Think about your possible reactions in relation to the following questions:

- What is the worst that could happen?
- What is the best that could happen?
- Why do you believe this?
- What evidence do you have both for and against your belief?
- What alternative beliefs are there?
- Are you jumping to conclusions?
- Are you exaggerating or over-generalizing?
- Do you have past experience of this sort of situation that you can draw on for help?
- How do you think you come across to this person – is your body language off-putting or creating a barrier?
- How do you think this person is feeling? Could he be every bit as nervous as you?

This exercise is designed to get you to look at the problem from all angles rather than go straight to your 'default setting' of being anxious and self-conscious when faced with a difficult social situation.

Also, consider that while you are consumed with your own emotions, this new person may also be feeling awkward, embarrassed and nervous about meeting you! If you can begin to step outside your own self-awareness and utilize the amazing sensitivity and empathy you have for other people, it can help to take the focus away from your own feelings and create rapport with the people you are interacting with.

Keep an open mind about the situation. Unless someone actually comes out and says directly to you something like 'I think you're really stupid', then you have absolutely no way of reading their thoughts or assuming you know what they think. Let's go back to the example on p. 79 and consider the following possibilities:

- Perhaps this man is annoyed with the host for dragging him away from an important business conversation and it has nothing to do with you.
- Perhaps he's just had some bad news and is upset.
- Perhaps he's experiencing physical pain.
- Perhaps he's shy too and is feeling nervous and embarrassed about meeting you.
- Perhaps he's a really nice person and you will get along just fine.
- Perhaps you are judging him unfairly even before you have met him.
- Perhaps he's asked to meet you and is really looking forward to it.

The point is, you simply don't know what is going through this person's mind. Apart from the fact that it is simply not fair to prejudge people, you are creating unnecessary barriers and spoiling your chance to make new friends and acquaintances. You may already realize how destructive social anxiety can be, but by changing your perspective and thinking through alternative beliefs, you can start to loosen the hold that shyness has over your whole being. Imagine how wonderful it would feel to be free of all that self-consciousness and embarrassment and be able to focus on the people you are with – and actually enjoy social occasions!

Try to avoid making 'rules' for yourself, such as 'I must go up to people and introduce myself' or 'I ought to be able to speak to the group about my project'. Also avoid taking extremist views, such as 'no one ever understands how I feel' or 'they always make fun of me'. Extremist views, by their very nature, are unlikely to be true. By making rules for yourself, you are not only pressurizing yourself unnecessarily, but your rules (as well as your extremist thoughts) will be tied in to your underlying beliefs and assumptions. Therefore neither is conducive to challenging your beliefs and finding alternatives.

Fear

One of our primary emotions is fear, an effective survival mecha-nism originating in the limbic system of the brain of mammals that evolved over 200 million years ago. When we feel fear, we feel the effects of the release of adrenalin on our nervous system. This is the fight or flight response that causes our heart to beat faster and increases blood flow to the muscles.

Throughout our evolutionary history, we have responded sub-consciously to threats in the environment such as poisonous spiders and snakes, or predatory animals such as lions. We also fear stimuli connected with disease, such as substances that are perceived as dirty, and animals associated with decay (for example, maggots and worms). Phobias such as arachnophobia (the fear of spiders) can occur when we experience irrational fears because our conscious reasoning is overruled by subconscious conditioning.

As we discussed at the beginning of this book, humans evolved in social groups that were vital for survival. The fear, apprehen-sion, anxiety and self-awareness we feel in social situations may be related to the evolution of social skills that were necessary for cooperation within the group – failure could result in being cast out from the group and left at the mercy of the natural world. This gives a real evolutionary basis for social anxiety and an explanation for the feelings we have.

Fear is usually experienced as a rush of emotion, a torrent of hormones coursing through your bloodstream triggered by your nervous system; in other words, an 'adrenalin rush'. If you think of the physical feelings that fear produces as simply a cocktail of chemicals coursing through your body, you can rationalize that this feeling will pass. You can decide to 'feel the fear and do it anyway' (the title of a wonderful book by Susan Jeffers), knowing that this feeling is simply an ancient biological reaction which is out of context in the situation you are faced with. You are not being attacked by a lion in a life or death struggle, you are simply dining with friends!

You can choose to ignore the physical feeling of fear. Recognize that this ancient response is inappropriate in your current situation and decide instead to act on your will and your logic, knowing that the physical feeling of fear will dissipate. It's very much like 'mind over matter'.

Fake it till you make it

While you are slowly working on changing your beliefs and experimenting with new behaviours, you can also take another approach and 'fake it till you make it'.

This approach was seen in the early twentieth century, when the Viennese psychiatrist Jacob Levy Moreno developed psychodrama (using drama as a form of group therapy) to help his patients work through their crises and conflicts. The principles of psychodrama and improvisational acting were used again in the 1990s when Alexander Avila developed ImprovTherapy to help shy people improve their social confidence and bring out repressed parts of the personality. He used this approach mainly to help shy people find and develop romantic relationships.

The main benefit in faking your behaviour is that you find a way to cut into the destructive vicious circles that maintain your social anxiety. For example, imagine you are invited to go out for drink with some people from another office at work. You don't really know these people and you feel that you don't really belong, you feel different. As you begin to worry that you will not have anything to say or that you will do something wrong, you start to feel panicky and sweaty, and your mind goes completely blank. You become painfully self-conscious, start to avoid eye contact and say little because you're afraid of making a fool of yourself. All this reinforces your belief that you don't belong with these people. And crucially, this vicious circle is maintained not only from within your own mind, but from outside too. As you start to withdraw into your self-consciousness, avoiding conversation or eye contact, the other people in the group will start to ignore you and talk among themselves, making you feel even more isolated and different.

Now imagine that you recognize this pattern in your behaviour, challenge your beliefs and adopt the alternative that, in fact, these people invited you along because they actually enjoy your company. Despite your nervousness, you begin to overrule your default setting – you smile, adopt an open body posture and make small contributions here and there to the conversation. As the other people in the group continue to include you and interact with you, you begin to relax and believe that actually these people *really do* enjoy your company and are interested in you. The result is that although you initially 'faked' your uncharacteristically sociable behaviour, the positive feedback you gained from the other people in the group increased your confidence and self-esteem, quelled your nerves and allowed you to take part and feel included.

This approach may seem daunting and will take some courage to try at first, but think of it as a scientific experiment. If it doesn't work particularly well the first time, don't be put off. A scientific experiment demands replication in order to determine whether or not the theory it is testing is true, and so you need to try this method several times and monitor the results to see if it is something that will help you.

11

Making changes

As well as challenging your beliefs, changing your perspective on things and finding alternatives, actually doing things differently can be very productive and will help build your confidence. Try to carry out small experiments, such as smiling and keeping an open posture when you meet people. Monitor how this makes you feel and whether it helps to dissipate your nervousness, and also notice whether other people react to you differently. These small changes can start a cascade of positive feedbacks that will propel you towards the big transformations you want to make in your life.

As you make small changes and begin to open up your mind to alternative perspectives, there is an important biological mechanism at work – you are actually altering the structure of your brain and creating new neural pathways. This is the natural mechanism responsible for learning and memory. It is called neural plasticity and is the key to making permanent changes in your life.

Neural pathways

Our brains and minds hold the patterns formed in our neurons, which we have been developing since childhood and are the basis of our personality and behaviour. Our neural networks hold all our unique memories and associations, some of them very firmly established or entrenched with deep neural pathways, others more superficial and easily altered. These networks are the result of repetitions and habits of thought so that every time we think or behave in a certain way, these pathways are reinforced and our behaviour becomes ingrained. Our brains do not distinguish between good and bad, healthy and unhealthy behaviour – they simply form a pattern in our brain as a result of habitual thinking. The old adage 'repetition is the mother of learning' is true.

You might think that after a lifetime of reinforcing the behaviour associated with social anxiety and shyness it would be impossible to change these neural networks. After all, they must be deeply entrenched in your brain. But the brain shows an incredible ability to rewire itself in response to new experiences and learning, even in adults. This neural plasticity has been demonstrated experimentally time and time again.

Creating new neural pathways

Just as you would blaze a new trail through the undergrowth in the jungle, it is possible to create new neural pathways and subsequently to make permanent changes to your behaviour. And similarly when old trails are not used and maintained by people walking down them, they become lost in the undergrowth. In your brain, the process of creating new neural pathways is called *synaptogenesis* and involves the creation and maintenance of new synapses (or of new gaps) between existing neurons.

This happens naturally every time we learn something new or create a new memory. But the problem is that unless these new neural pathways are used and reinforced on a regular basis, they will not become permanent and the old pathways will become the 'default' setting in your brain.

In order to establish new neural networks and change ingrained behaviour, continued stimulation of these networks is essential. This process is called *long-term potentiation* and was proposed by Donald Hebb in 1949 (Hebb's rule). Neurons that are repeatedly fired or stimulated form a long-term network of connections. This is the opposite of a process called *long-term depression*, which reduces the strength of the synapse between neurons when they are not used for long periods. Long-term potentiation and long-term depression work together, continuing to enable learning, memory and changes in behaviour to occur. This is the basis of neural plasticity and it opens up extraordinary opportunities to improve our lives and make permanent changes to our behaviour.

It can take several months for new ways of behaving to become permanent habits because of the length of time new neural networks take to establish themselves, mature and strengthen. Remember that every time you repeat an old or unwanted behaviour, you simply strengthen the old neural networks associated with it and perpetuate the behaviour you are trying to change. You need to strengthen the neural networks associated with your *new* behaviour in order to create the mature synapses in your brain that will lead to permanent changes. Be patient and give yourself time. Repeat your goals and implement your action plans on a daily basis over a period of several months.

Setting goals

It is important to set goals for yourself and to plan how you will make changes in your life. It is probably better to tackle some of the easier aspects of your social anxiety first and work up to the more difficult problems.

It is crucial to *write out* your goals and your action plans. By writing them down you crystallize your thoughts and make a mental commitment to them. Writing them down forces you to be specific and identifies the strengths and weaknesses of your plan.

Goals should include all areas of your life, since your whole life is affected, although some areas will need more work than others. When you plan your goals, you should strive to balance the following aspects of your life:

- physical
- intellectual/mental
- social/relationships
- spiritual/personal growth
- financial
- time management.

Break your goals down into manageable chunks. Each goal is a step along the path to making the changes you want. Your goals should be specific, realistic, time sensitive, and capable of change.

Specific

State exactly what you want. If you want to develop the confidence to make new friends, state exactly how you will achieve this. Will you meet people on the internet to begin with and gradually work up to 'real' meeting? Or will you join the local rambling group and start developing social contacts? Get as much detail as possible. Vague statements won't work; you need to be specific and really know what you want. Be concise and really prioritize what it is you want to achieve.

Realistic

If you want to find a romantic partner, do you have a workable plan as to how you'll achieve this? If you're not going to meet someone in your local area, what will you do to open up the opportunity to meet new people? Your goals have to be realistic. You really can achieve extraordinary things but you have to have a plan as to how you'll get there one step at a time.

Time sensitive

When do you want to achieve a particular goal? Vague open-ended statements won't do either. You have to have a deadline or your natural tendency will be to leave it and let other things take priority. It will be all too easy to melt into the background again and put things off for another time unless you have a realistic time frame – for example, you could set a goal to join the ramblers' group in the next two weeks.

You should have short-term, medium-term and long-term goals. Short-term goals could be things you set yourself every day and will become part of your daily life. They could include things like keeping a journal, smiling at people you meet and practising open body postures. Medium-term goals could be anything from six months to several years and include things like making new friends or finding a romantic partner. Long-term goals could span the rest of your life. Take time to plan out your 'map' for achieving your goals and review them often. Where do you want to be in six months, a year, five years?

Capable of change

Things change, circumstances alter our plans for better or worse and sometimes we simply change our minds about things. Your goals must be firm but not set in stone. They have to be capable of changing and adapting. You might really want to join the ramblers' group, but you've decided to take an evening class in watercolour painting instead. That's OK! Your plans can develop and metamorphose into different things and so they should. You're not a failure because you didn't achieve a particular goal. You have to build in a degree of flexibility to your plans and allow for those twists and turns that life hands out sometimes.

Making a plan of action

Once you have a specific, realistic, time-sensitive goal, you need a plan of action. How are you going to achieve it? Say your goal is to start a conversation with someone at your sister's party. How will you do it? Will you simply walk up to them, smile and say hello, or will you prepare a little beforehand by finding out about them from your sister, or will you ask for an introduction? Having a plan of action is having the intention to actually do something toward achieving your goal.

Rewards

When you are depressed or unhappy, it is important to create sensory experiences to make you feel good. Buy yourself some flowers, or better still, grow some in the garden or in pots. Have a little treat occasionally, even if it's only a box of chocolates or a long soak in the bath with a glass of wine. You're worth a little pampering. Take time to watch a sunset or sit by a river and watch the world go by. Take time every day to remember all the wonderful things in life and be grateful for what you have.

Rewards keep you moving toward your goals and make the whole thing more fun, so plan in some rewards along the way to keep you on track. Buy yourself a treat when you've plucked up the courage to go to the office party, or treat yourself to an ice cream when you've managed to join in the conversation over lunch.

Review

You should evaluate your goals as you go along. Are they still valid? Are you on track? Find out if they need a 'tweak' here and there to enable you to make progress. Ideally, review your goals every day. Read them aloud and reaffirm them to yourself. Repeat your goals often to make them a real part of your life. Have them at the forefront of your mind every day. Live them fully. It is an idea to set aside a few minutes at the same time every day to think about and repeat your goals. Even go to the trouble of writing them out again every day. Your goals are the vehicle for achieving the changes you want to make and they have a fundamental importance in your life. Spend time on them. Most people spend more time on their shopping list than they do planning their life.

Look over your goals and evaluate how you're doing at least once a week. Time spent in this way is invaluable and could save years of blundering along on the wrong path. It will keep you focused and inspire you to keep going if you remind yourself about what it is you are working toward. It will help you to keep your eyes on the horizon and see the bigger picture ... see your new-found confidence unfolding. Have a special file for your ongoing goals as well as your lists of things you want to do and of who you want to become. Make it your own private place where you are in touch with your true self, your desires, your dreams and your mission in life.

Time-related goals

Your subconscious mind will interpret the words of your goals literally, so you must take care to impress upon it exactly the details of what you want. Hence the need for specific, time-related goals. Personal goals such as changes to your personality should be made in the present tense, as if they were already happening: 'Every day I am becoming more and more confident, I am rejecting negative thoughts about myself'. Your subconscious will act on this as if it's happening now and make gradual improvements every day. There is no conflict there. If, however, it is for some vague time in the future – 'I will become more confident' – then your subconscious will simply wait for the time to act and do nothing to help you achieve it now.

Other goals should be time related: 'I will join the ramblers' group by Saturday'. Some people suggest all goals should be in the present tense, as if you had already achieved them. To me this conflicts with the truth, so that your conscious mind will not accept and believe it enough to allow your subconscious to accept and act upon it.

Helping your subconscious

One way to help saturate your subconscious with ideas and attract the things you want is to make an audio tape or CD of your goals and aspirations. It is similar to a self-hypnosis tape. You write out your goals and the things you want to achieve or change in your life and record them on to a tape to play in the car, at the gym, out walking or whenever you have a few spare minutes in the day. Best of all, fill the tape up completely, repeating the same thing over and over, and play it when you go to bed at night. Your subconscious will pick up the message while you sleep and strive to change attitudes or behaviour and create the circumstances you want.

Use your imagination

Your imagination is the most powerful ally you have when it comes to making changes to your life. Everything around us begins with a thought. The everyday things you use, the creative art you see and the books you read all began as a thought in someone's mind. You can make the changes you want in your imagination. And by focusing on them, believing in them and taking action, you can create those changes in reality.

This process is called *creative visualization*. Athletes use this technique to achieve success. They vividly imagine themselves sprinting to the finish line and rehearse the whole race in their minds; step by step. Great golfers practise in their minds; they feel and see themselves hitting the ball with precision. You can use creative visualization to add power to your goals and reinforce the new neural pathways associated with the changes you want to make.

If you want to feel confident around other people, imagine yourself behaving with confidence – vividly imagine how it feels to be a confident person. Use the power of your emotions and feel excited and elated at having all that confidence, bring it to life ... imagine what the new confident you looks like, see yourself interacting with others and meeting new people without a care in the world. Rehearsing in your imagination is the first step to achieving success.

12
Coping with stress and anxiety

While you are challenging your thinking and experimenting with new ways of behaving, you can implement various simple ways of reducing stress and anxiety. This can only help to maximize your success and help you to feel calm and in control. Chronic stress and anxiety can be very debilitating and it is important to reduce their effects, not only to help you overcome social anxiety, but for your general health and well-being.

Stress for our ancestors was a survival mechanism. The stress response evolved as a way to respond to threats such as predators – the flight or fight response – but in today's modern world, these sorts of threats are uncommon. Our natural biochemistry 'overreacts' and produces more of the stress hormone, cortisol, than we actually need – resulting in the build-up of cortisol in our bodies known as 'chronic stress'.

The physical stress response

Stress signals (including emotional stress signals) are sent to the hypothalamus at the base of the brain. Through a series of hormonal messages, the stress hormone cortisol is then released from the adrenal glands, situated just above the kidneys. The release of cortisol into the bloodstream gives the body a surge of energy for the flight or fight response.

The body is put on alert; hearing and sense of smell become more acute, muscles tense ready for activity, and heart and breathing rates increase. Blood pressure elevates and blood flow is diverted to the brain and muscles ready for action. This sudden release of cortisol is designed for a quick response to danger and once the cortisol is used up by running or fighting, the body quickly returns to normal.

However, problems occur when we do not use up the excess cortisol. Chronic stress puts us at risk from a multitude of conditions, such as the following:

- The heart muscle may be damaged and arrhythmias occur from constantly elevated levels of stress hormones.
- Brain cells can be irreversibly destroyed due to surges in cortisol.
- Muscle spasms and tension may occur, causing back pain, stiff aching limbs and headaches.
- Increased cortisol interferes with glucose metabolism, increasing the risks of heart disease, stroke, cataracts, diabetes, obesity, insulin resistance and premature ageing.
- Chronic stress puts pressure on the immune system and can result in lowered resistance to infections such as colds, flu, asthma, allergies and other infections.
- And importantly, stress lowers our emotional strength to cope with life and makes us vulnerable to anxiety and depression.

Chronic stress can cause untold damage to your physical and emotional health and also dampens your spirit for life.

Reducing stress

Balance your life. Too much work and not enough relaxation is not good for you; neither is not having enough stimulation or projects that challenge you. Exercise is one of the best ways to de-stress and discharge cortisol from your body, and you can see from the following list the other amazing benefits exercise brings. Exercise:

- reduces nervousness and anxiety;
- improves your mental clarity;
- elevates mood;
- increases self-esteem and self-confidence;
- increases energy and reduces fatigue;
- increases the production of endorphins, helping you feel calm;
- helps you sleep better;
- improves strength and stamina;
- improves muscle tone;

- improves joint flexibility and suppleness;
- strengthens back muscles and eases back pain;
- strengthens heart muscle;
- improves lung function;
- improves digestion;
- increases resting metabolic rate, helping to regulate body weight;
- slows down the ageing process and helps you look better;
- reduces the risk of heart disease;
- lowers blood pressure;
- reduces the risk of osteoporosis and increases bone density;
- reduces the risk of mature onset diabetes;
- improves your insulin/blood glucose mechanism;
- rebalances cholesterol to healthy levels;
- feels good!

Just a long walk three times a week will help reduce cortisol levels, improve your level of fitness and increase your mental and physical well-being. Here are a few other ideas, which may also help to conquer stress:

- Manage your time effectively and prioritize urgent and important tasks.
- Set priorities and realize you can't do everything.
- De-clutter your life and try to reduce the amount of 'stuff to do' that is not important.
- Value your time and insist that others value your time too.
- Don't become a domestic slave – get the family to help with household chores.
- Spend more time with the people and the pets you love.
- Be daft once in a while and have fun.
- Take stress seriously and tackle the causes of stress in your life.
- Make time in your daily routine for formal relaxation. Try yoga or meditation.
- Have a long soak in a bubble bath.
- Take some long deep breaths to feel calm instantly.
- Invest in a massager to help de-stress your muscles after a hard day.
- Have a good long belly laugh every day – laughter *really is* the best medicine.

- Have a good cry – sometimes you just have to get it out of your system.
- Curl up with a good book for the whole afternoon – and don't feel guilty about it.

Chronic resentment and grumbling anger seething away below the surface is a major cause of chronic stress, so deal with it, and have it out with whoever is adding to your stress – then forget it and get on with your day.

Our need for nature

We evolved genetically to balance stressful periods of hunting and dealing with wild predators with periods of relaxation and socializing. Our ancestors were also living among nature with green grass, trees and plants, clean water and pure air, not having to contend with mile upon mile of barren concrete and the polluted atmosphere of our modern towns and cities. It is very important to reconnect with nature on a regular basis if we are to experience balance and harmony and beat the stresses of modern life. A long walk in the country or along the beach can do wonders for your soul as well as your physical and emotional health.

Coping with people who cause stress

Other people can cause stress and difficulties for all of us. If you are shy, coping with such people can be exceedingly difficult – but it is perfectly possible. Awkward people are everywhere, and it can be a complicated business trying to understand and deal with someone's negative or unhealthy attitudes and just plain bad behaviour. So how can you reduce or eliminate the detrimental effects of difficult people?

Well, one obvious way is to avoid them. Sometimes it *is* possible with acquaintances and even work colleagues for you to simply distance yourself from them and never see them again. However, if this is not possible and the person causing you (and probably everyone else) problems is someone like your boss, your neighbour or your mother-in-law, whom you inevitably have to see from time to time, then you have to find ways to deal with them – for the sake of your health, and your sanity!

Changing your reaction

Often, simply being more assertive will solve the problem (see Chapter 13). But there are also other ways to cope. One way is to change your reaction. Think of an incident where you have had problems with somebody. Replay the incident in your mind and identify the aspects of the other person's behaviour that are causing you problems. Note the way you react. Perhaps your boss is overly aggressive and you are unable to stand up to him or her. Now think of somebody who does deal well with the boss. How would they approach the situation? Replay the incident in your mind, imagine that you are like this person and change your usual reaction. If you always back down, imagine standing up for yourself and replay this new scenario over and over in your mind as you did with the creative visualization technique we discussed earlier. Practise your new reaction in your imagination.

When you imagine the situation, see the other person as inferior to you because of his attitude, see him as physically smaller than you and realize that his behaviour is more to do with deficiencies in his own character than a personal attack on you. You could also imagine him or her having to do the same things we all have to do. Imagine your boss in her pyjamas, cleaning her teeth, struggling with the children or shopping for groceries – in other words see her on the same level as everyone else. We are all human beings, and nobody is 'better' or more entitled to be here than anyone else. You'll be amazed how this will give you the strength to change your perspective on the situation and help you to modify your reaction.

This change may just be the catalyst you need to begin making improvements in your relationships with difficult people. Social interactions with particular people tend to follow the same pattern every time. If your mother-in-law bullies you and you always sit back and take it, this behaviour and this pattern will continue, but if you change your attitude and your reaction, you catch her out – you suddenly become unpredictable. This is often a turning point in transforming relationships with other people.

Adopt this technique with anyone who is awkward or difficult to deal with.

Jane

After her husband left her, Jane was having genuine problems with her finances and was required to attend appointments with her bank manager, Mr Williams, on a regular basis. She found him extremely intimidating and felt that he was abusing his position to exert power over her. He was overbearing, rude and generally obstructive of her efforts to solve her financial problems. Jane often left Mr Williams's office in tears and it was dragging her down. When Jane heard about this technique, she imagined herself reacting to her bank manager as her friend Sandra would have done. She replayed different scenarios in her mind, changing her reaction and becoming more assertive. She imagined Mr Williams doing mundane chores like cutting the lawn, putting out the rubbish bags and arguing with his wife (who always got the better of him!). She 'demoted' him in her mind, no longer felt intimidated by his position and reasoned that the sort of behaviour he displayed showed immaturity and was nothing to do with her personally. By visualizing a different reaction before their next meeting, she amazed herself by calmly telling him that she was unhappy with his proposals for dealing with her account and that she would like to discuss it with his superior. That one conversation made all the difference and Mr Williams suddenly became remarkably more respectful and accommodating with her. Their meetings became easier and Jane found renewed confidence in dealing with awkward people.

Generally, people don't set out to be awkward, but somewhere along the line their intentions can determine the way they behave. For instance, people who want to 'get the job done' and are under pressure can seem controlling with others, but when the pressure is off they may be more easygoing; people who need to be appreciated can often be forceful, brash and attention seeking, and so on. Sometimes when people's needs are not met, they become difficult and awkward. Their behaviour is determined by their own perception of what they believe is important at the time; it is not a personal reflection on you. However, you can reduce the impact of difficult behaviour directed at you by changing your own perspective.

Using dissociation

You may remember our discussion about changing your focus, or dissociation. In this technique, you observe yourself from a third party perspective and see yourself from outside, while still having thoughts and feelings about your emotional reactions and behaviour. You can use dissociation techniques to distance yourself or change your perspective when dealing with difficult people.

- **You can reduce its importance.** Compare the problems you are having now to more difficult times in your life. How do the problems you are having with this person compare to a tragedy such as losing a loved one or being paralysed in an accident?
- **Will it matter a year from now?** Project yourself into the future and decide what difference this problem will make. If it's not crucial to your future happiness or success – it's not worth worrying about it now.
- **Nothing lasts for ever.** Your meeting and even your relationship or association with this person will not last for ever. Think about problem people you've had to deal with in the past – their time came and went just as this time in your life will pass too. Project yourself into the future when your association with this person is finished with; it may help you gain perspective.
- **Change the significance.** Change the meaning of the whole problem and think of the ways in which this difficult person is helping you to develop your inner strength, patience and tolerance, and improve your communication skills. With hindsight, Jane was grateful for the insight she gained by having to deal with the problems she'd been having with her bank manager. In the end, it boosted her confidence and allowed her to apply the techniques to other difficult relationships. Now her friend is more thoughtful toward her and her brother no longer takes her for granted as much as he did. In turn Jane has a new perspective which has considerably reduced her shyness in social situations.
- **Look for opportunities.** Every problem throws up an opportunity to learn and develop as a person if we look for it. Find the positive aspects of every 'problem' and ask 'What can I learn from this?' Remember that gold, silver and diamonds are

found in muddy water, dirt and rocks – you just have to look for them.

By using dissociation techniques, you can reinterpret the behaviour of difficult people and improve your skill at dealing with awkward social interactions. What you learn from dealing with difficult people will develop your character, make you stronger and give you experience that you can apply in other areas of your life.

13

Increasing self-esteem and confidence

Definitions of self-esteem vary, but all agree that high self-esteem means that we appreciate ourselves and believe that we are worthwhile. It means having a positive attitude toward yourself, valuing yourself and believing in your competence and abilities. It also means being in control of your own life and being able to achieve success in your own way, rather than following the dictates of society or of other people. Having high self-esteem also means that we compare ourselves favourably with others and that we do not consider ourselves inferior to anyone else. It involves our ability to think, to deal with life's adversities and to be happy whatever our circumstances.

Self-esteem begins to develop in childhood and is affected by our upbringing, our choice of career, our circle of friends and choice of partner. Certain life events can affect our self-esteem; often these are temporary, but sometimes the effects are long-lasting. We can all suffer loss and rejection, accidents, career setbacks and any number of adversities, but our self-esteem and our outlook on life will make a crucial difference in how we deal with ups and downs. A healthy self-esteem can cushion us and allow us to get through the downturns.

But high self-esteem can never be 'given' to someone by another person or by society. It must be sought and earned – self-esteem is shaped throughout our lives and it is perfectly possible to increase your self-esteem if you are motivated to do so.

How's your self-esteem?

The way we live our lives is profoundly affected by the way we view and feel about ourselves. Our view of ourselves fluctuates constantly and is influenced by events and encounters with other people, as well as by our own constant judgement and evaluation of ourselves. It is when our judgement of ourselves becomes overly dependent on what other people think of us, and when we evaluate and constantly compare ourselves unfavourably to other people, that our self-esteem declines. Ask yourself the following questions:

- Do I like myself?
- Am I proud of *who* I am?
- Am I proud of what I'm doing with my life?
- Am I a decent human being?
- Do I deserve to be loved?
- Do I deserve to be happy?
- Do I accept my faults and limitations?
- Do I recognize that nobody is perfect – that we all have our faults?
- Do I believe that my opinions are as valid as anybody else's?
- Do I believe I am as good as anybody else?
- Do I treat myself and others with respect?
- Am I committed to self-improvement?
- Do I take responsibility for myself and my actions?

If you have a healthy measure of self-esteem, you should be able to answer yes to all (or most!) of the above. We all have our own strengths and limitations; we are all different. We may well wish to change aspects of ourselves and it is healthy to strive for self-improvement, but a healthy self-esteem is also based on self-understanding and self-acceptance.

Increasing self-esteem

So how can you improve your self-esteem? First of all, realize that you are not alone. Many people suffer low self-esteem, whether or not they are shy. It is a common problem in a modern society that generates such impossibly high expectations. We are bombarded on a daily basis with images of glamorous, successful people with whom we compare ourselves unfavourably. We are expected to perform flawlessly in our careers, be the perfect friend and partner and sparkle socially. But nobody is perfect, and we all make mistakes; this is a normal part of being human. To build a healthy self-esteem, you need to gain perspective and judge your goals and aspirations independently of society and other people at large. The only real success is in being able to live your life in your own way. Learn to disregard what others are doing and evaluate your own character and behaviour on its own merits. Only *you* can be the judge of your character and your own life ...

Consider the following suggestions for increasing self-esteem:

- **Learn something new.** Take a course or try something new to stretch yourself and discover your talents and abilities.
- **Look after yourself.** Eat sensibly, keep fit and get enough rest and sleep. It's hard to feel good about yourself if you're feeling fat, frumpy and worn out.
- **Pamper yourself.** Make a list of all the things you like for yourself and don't feel guilty about it.
- **Reward yourself.** Have a day off now and again just to do something for yourself or buy yourself a little treat.
- **Avoid negative people or situations.** Spend time on experiences that make you feel good and avoid people, places and situations that make you feel bad about yourself.
- **Talk to yourself.** Celebrate the wonderful things in your life and point out all your best qualities by positive self-talk. If you find yourself saying things like 'I'm stupid' or 'I'll never be able to achieve my dreams', stop yourself and turn these statements around: 'I'm perfectly intelligent' and 'I can do anything I put my mind to'.
- **Have realistic expectations.** Take a reality test. Are you expecting too much of yourself or trying to please everybody? Try to be happy with being 'good enough' once in a while.
- **Forgive yourself and others.** Don't punish yourself or other people for ever over mistakes and errors of judgement. Turn them into positive opportunities to improve and learn.
- **List 50 things you like about yourself.** List all the aspects of your character, your looks, and the things you have done with your life that you like and are proud of. Add something new to the list every day.
- **Ask for support.** Stop struggling to do everything yourself at home or at work and get others to take responsibility for themselves. Your time is important too.

- **Learn how to be more assertive.** You have a right to stand up for your wants and needs, so learn how to develop an assertive attitude.
- **Get involved.** Your contribution is as valuable as anybody else's. Take part in community activities and social events as an equally important member of the group.
- **Reach out.** We all need other people and making new friends can happen at all stages of life. Be the first to reach out to others and cultivate relationships – your friendship is a valuable commodity to other people, so don't deny them the pleasure of your company.
- **Don't hide away.** Don't use shyness as an excuse to hide away and avoid social contact. Take up the challenge and vow to conquer your nervousness – make it a serious project in your life.
- **Take responsibility.** Don't wait for other people or circumstances to make you feel better about yourself – accept responsibility for your actions and for your own happiness.
- **Listen to criticism.** Evaluate what others have to say about you in an objective way. Everyone is entitled to their opinion but that doesn't mean that criticism is justified. What other people think about you is their business – have the strength of character to rely on your own judgement of yourself.

Becoming more confident

Confident people are generally self-assured and self-reliant. They believe they can succeed and are convinced that they have the ability to achieve their goals. Confident people are not deterred by difficulties or setbacks and embrace life's challenges.

If you have poor self-confidence, you are likely to feel anxious, helpless and stressed, and that you lack control. The less control you feel you have, the more anxious you become and the less confident you will be. However, you can cut into this negative spiral by focusing on your strengths, your skills and your ability to cope with a situation – even when you are unable to change it. You may feel more confident in some areas of your life than others; for example, it is not unusual to find someone who is successful and confident in their career but less confident in their personal relationships. Even if you are shy in social situations, you can still be self-confident in other areas of your life, and there are ways you can increase your overall confidence that can lead to reduced anxiety in social situations.

Think about the benefits of having more confidence and why this is such an important goal for you. Consider what makes achieving this goal so difficult at the moment. Then think about the strengths you have and what you can do to improve your level of confidence – the section on self-esteem should help you refocus on your strengths.

Think about your body language, the impression you make on people and the subconscious messages you are sending out. It is estimated that as much as 80 per cent of the impression you create comes from your body language, so it is worth paying special attention to your posture, facial expression, eye contact and gestures as they can speak much more effectively than the words you say. While you should avoid controlling your body language in an unnatural way and end up looking like a 'fake', you can subtly adopt an open, friendly posture to make you appear more confident than you really feel. It takes a stranger just 30 seconds to form an impression of someone, so make sure you smile, make eye contact and create a positive, upbeat impression – that alone can make you feel good. And there are many more things you can do to boost both your confidence and your self-esteem.

Tips for boosting your confidence

The following suggestions may help you feel more confident in specific situations:

- Confident breathing is slow and deep, so catch yourself 'hyperventilating' because of nervousness and take some slow, deep breaths to calm yourself down.
- Think of a phrase that will help you through a difficult moment, such as 'whatever happens, I can do this ...'
- Dress in an appropriate way that expresses your personality and take time to be well groomed for a difficult occasion. If you are confident that you look your best, you can forget about your appearance and concentrate on the people you are with.

- If you feel yourself becoming tense, take a deep breath and relax your neck and shoulders. Try to do this every 15 minutes or so to give you a more confident stance.
- If you're feeling nervous, take a second or two to think about someone or something you love and appreciate. Think warm, lovely thoughts and refocus your feelings.
- Imagine you are cuddling and stroking a pet cat or dog, heave a big sigh and visualize yourself calming down.
- Imagine yourself being enveloped in the arms of someone you love.
- Wear a scent that you like. If you feel yourself becoming anxious, take another sniff; it can help your mood and confidence. Lavender is thought to be relaxing, while jasmine promotes confidence and strength.

Here are some other things that you can do that may help to boost your confidence generally:

- A clean and tidy home will have an uplifting effect on your mood since how you live is a reflection of your inner state. Stepping around clutter and putting up with dirt erodes your confidence. If your self-esteem is low, then you may be letting things slip at home. Have a sort-out and get the family to do their fair share around the house.
- Keep a little book of quotations and pictures that make you feel good. An inspirational quote can do wonders for your self-esteem and confidence.
- Sit somewhere comfortable and quiet, take some deep breaths and close your eyes. Imagine you have a black velvet eye mask on and empty your mind of everything for a few minutes. Just picture black velvet ...
- Make a special audio tape or CD with songs that make you feel happy, inspired, hopeful and upbeat. Music can change your mood instantly and help you feel more positive and confident.
- Go for a long walk and give yourself a pep talk. Remember all your strengths and amazing qualities and give yourself a lift.
- Participate in voluntary activities and community projects such as helping the elderly or disabled or raising funds for a village

sports field. These altruistic activities will give your confidence a real boost.

- Develop confidence based on your inner qualities rather than on your accomplishments. True confidence comes not from the things we achieve in life but from the self-assurance we feel when we are happy and satisfied with who we are.

Even confident people have doubts about themselves. Confidence is not fixed but can waver with moods, level of energy and motivation; it ebbs and flows. Confidence can come in different guises. Many people appear to be confident when really they are feeling nervous or unsure of themselves. Conversely, others can appear awkward or lacking in confidence when in fact they have a solid inner confidence and don't worry about the sort of temporary embarrassments that happen to everyone. Very often it is difficult to tell if somebody is confident or not, and one of the most useful strategies is to behave as if you were more confident than you feel. The feedback and the reactions you get from other people will actually increase your confidence.

Reducing self-consciousness

Self-consciousness can dominate your attention and make it difficult to think of anything else but your inner experience. It can affect you in any social situation, even with people you know well. When you feel self-conscious, you feel conspicuous and vulnerable. You may suddenly become aware of all the symptoms of social anxiety, such as feeling nervous or not being able to think straight, which may in turn lead to self-protective behaviours such as melting into the background, disappearing into the kitchen at parties or, worse, avoiding social situations altogether.

Being self-conscious ruins your confidence, gets in the way of you being spontaneous and prevents your true personality from shining through. It also prevents you from participating fully in social interactions and concentrating on what you are doing, since your mind is focused on your inner world. You might find yourself becoming clumsy or awkward and not able to follow the conversation because you are not concentrating fully on what is going on around you.

The best way to reduce self-consciousness is to practise focusing your attention on what is going on around you and the people you are with, instead of being absorbed by your inner world. It will take conscious effort at first. Make it a project to find out about the people you are with. You could try to guess what they do for a living; think about their families and their homes; try to work out how they are feeling or what interests them. The point is to take the attention away from how you are feeling and your own self-consciousness and deliberately turn your attention outward.

Aim eventually to achieve a balance between focusing on your own feelings and on matters outside yourself. If you sense yourself becoming anxious and self-conscious, quickly turn your attention to something interesting; compliment somebody on their cooking, an item of clothing or their sense of humour. Keep your thoughts positive and upbeat.

People watching

A great time to do this is when you're out shopping or travelling with other people, on a bus or a plane. Practise 'people watching' and develop curiosity about the world around you. Many people who are shy worry about doing things 'correctly', so while you are spending time watching other people, take the opportunity to note how everyone does things differently. People greet each other in different ways, move around in different ways and are generally far too preoccupied with what they are doing themselves to notice or care about what you are doing. It is probably only you who are so concerned about the impression you make – everybody else will happily accept you just the way you are.

Richard
Richard was shy, but also an extrovert. He longed to make new friends and join in socially but was crippled by nervousness and anxiety, tending to stay home every evening surfing the internet when what he really wanted was to be out socializing. Richard decided to take action as his nervousness was making him depressed and hopeless about his life. He decided that nobody could help him change – he had to do it for himself. He started by going to the local pub. At first he made no attempt to speak to anyone – other than to order a drink at the bar – but simply sat and took in his surroundings, gradually calming down and

getting used to a lively atmosphere. He knew he could escape whenever he wanted to and tended to sit hunched in the corner, avoiding eye contact with anyone, fearful of starting a conversation. It seemed that nobody noticed him. But after a few evenings, Richard began to consciously adjust his body language. He began to sit up, open up his chest and unfold his arms; he uncrossed his legs and mentally opened up, sending out welcoming signals. He practised looking at people and smiling when he caught their eye, and this simple change in his demeanour made him feel more confident in a social setting than he had for a very long time. People began responding to him instead of ignoring him. Within an hour of this change, an old gentleman approached him and began chatting about the football results. Richard was delighted and amazed at the way he was able to respond to this man and maintain an interesting conversation. Even more amazing was that by the end of the evening, two of the old gentleman's friends had joined them at the table and Richard was able to participate fully. He even told a few jokes! Richard went home that evening feeling much more confident and hopeful about his life. He had finally broken the ice and it felt uplifting. He knew he would be welcomed again at the pub and that his fears about making new friends were totally unfounded. Just a simple change in Richard's attitude and the non-verbal signals he gave to others had opened up a new world of opportunity.

Becoming more assertive

If you are shy, you are very unlikely to be assertive. Yet it is important to stand up for your rights, wants and needs (without violating those of others). Being assertive allows you to say no to unreasonable requests and it prevents people taking advantage of your good nature or taking you for granted.

Both aggressive and non-assertive or submissive behaviour often originate from low self-esteem. Self-esteem is your own evaluation of yourself; your worth as a person, and your beliefs about yourself as a competent, worthwhile human being. People who behave aggressively may give the impression of being confident and self-assured, but this can be a cover for insecurity and poor self-regard.

When you behave in a submissive or non-assertive way, you use a lot of nervous energy by worrying about upsetting others. Shy people are notoriously submissive, and yet by trying to behave more assertively, you can increase your self-esteem, improve self-confidence and allow yourself to make changes to your life.

Here are some suggestions to help you become more assertive:

- Be clear and concise about what you want. Avoid long rambling speeches that can cause confusion.
- Avoid justifying yourself. You don't have to explain yourself to anyone.
- Don't apologize when you ask for something. For example, 'I'm really sorry to bother you …' simply weakens your position.
- Give yourself time to consider things before you agree to them and get into the habit of saying, 'Let me think about it', or 'I'll have to check my diary'.
- Don't put yourself down by saying things like, 'I'm hopeless at this …'
- Use steady eye contact to reinforce your point. Submissive people often avoid eye contact and inadvertently give the other person control of the situation, while aggressive people tend to stare at their opponents and dominate.
- Use open body language and keep your head held up. Avoid nervous movements such as hand wringing or folded arms. Submissive people tend to curl up to protect themselves, assertive people stand up and face the world, and aggressive people lean forward and attack.

Above all, it helps to have solid goals and a plan that you are deeply committed to and passionate about. It will help you to be assertive when you have something to stand up for and something you believe in.

Being true to yourself

Are you continually fighting with your own personality and trying to be something that you can never become? If you believe that you are abnormal because you are shy, you may be forcing yourself to join in socially and adopt a more extrovert lifestyle than you are comfortable with, rather than learning to accept yourself and your natural character. You may have a tendency to introversion as part of your biological makeup and there is very little that you can do to change this. Consider the aspects of your personality that you cannot change – accept them and embrace them as part of *you*. You are unique and special just as you are; you don't need to fit in with other people's expectations or society's 'norms'.

Forcing yourself to change your basic personality will merely sap your energy and create frustration and despondency; it can even make you ill. Nurture yourself and learn to understand your true

My personality traits: For example, kindness, sensitivity, a positive attitude, maturity, etc.	
The things I like: Reading, exercise, learning something new, organizing events, animals, etc.	
The people I like and admire: For example, Albert Einstein for his insight and intelligence …	
The things I want to achieve: Such as a promotion at work, a sports car, a home by the sea, etc.	
My highest aspirations: For example, to run my own business …	

temperament. Recognize when you are pushing yourself to 'fit in' with what others expect of you, rather than doing the things that make you really happy. If you are to find success and meaning in your life, you have to follow your heart and be true to yourself.

One way to understand yourself better is to brainstorm! Quickly write down anything that comes to mind in the table on p. 109.

Now go through your lists and highlight the items that *really* matter to you. What would you do with your life if you won £5 million?

Here are some other ideas to help you stay true to yourself:

- **Value yourself.** Your personal value is based on *who you are* not *what you do*. Stop worrying about the labels people put on you and realize the important contribution you make to the world just by being yourself.

- **Challenge yourself.** Sometimes, to be able to follow your goals and dreams you have to push yourself. If you want that promotion at work or to meet someone special you have to be prepared to do whatever it takes to make it happen. Don't let shyness stop you from following your dreams. There will always be obstacles, hurdles and uncomfortable feelings to deal with but look upon them as exciting adventures, challenges and opportunities for personal growth.

- **Restore your energy.** Introverts need time alone to reflect, think and contemplate while extroverts need time to connect with family and friends and to draw energy from their surroundings. Take a walk in the country, meditate, read something inspirational, listen to music or meet up with friends for a chat, but find time every day to recharge your batteries in your own way. Don't wait until you are too tired and depleted before you take a break.

- **Create your own space.** It's important to have a personal space where you can express yourself or retreat from the world. If you live alone this is not usually a problem, but if you live with other people and have to share your space, try to make sure everyone has a little corner to themselves free of interruptions and demands.

- **Embrace change.** People who are happy create the changes they want; they don't let their circumstances or other people dictate what their life should be like.
- **Start with small changes.** Like ripples in a pond, changing one small thing in your life can make a big difference. Think about the things you want to change and take action today – even if it is just one small thing toward your goal.
- **You can't change anyone else.** The only changes you can make are to your own life. Accept people as they are.
- **Don't take life too seriously.** Don't forget about the fun things in life! Once in a while, throw caution to the wind and be spontaneous. Being shy and self-conscious can be exhausting, so play, be silly and lift your spirits – do five things today just for the fun of it!
- **Your life reflects your beliefs.** When you change your beliefs about the world, your life will also change. Believe wholeheartedly that you can be the person you want to be and that you can achieve your goals and aspirations, and you will be amazed how your life will begin to move in the direction you want.
- **Focus on the positive.** Focus your attention on the things you *want*, not on the things you *don't want*. Remember our discussion about neural networks and how we reinforce new pathways by repetition? Don't reinforce old, negative pathways; create exciting changes by focusing on the positive new pathways.
- **Follow your heart.** Life is too short to be miserable and unfulfilled … discover who you are and what you want out of life before it's too late. Doing what you love may not be the easiest option but it's better than accepting second best and having regrets.
- **Aim for the stars.** Human beings can achieve the most amazing things when they follow their dreams. Believe you can have the life you want and reach up towards your highest aspirations.
- **Take action.** Set your goals and have the courage to act. Take the plunge, do something *now* and you will find that action creates the motivation to continue.
- **Experiment.** If you're not sure what you want out of life, experiment and try new things. Take a risk now and again and before long you could discover an all-consuming passion that will take your life in a new direction.

14

Finding friends and romance

Even shy introverts who are uncomfortable with social interactions want and need a variety of relationships, whether it be a marriage partner, close friendships, work colleagues, acquaintances or the camaraderie of a community. Think about the social network you have now and consider how you might develop new relationships, rekindle old ones and extend your friendships. Do you want romance? More close friendships? To join or start a group of people with similar interests to your own? To be active in a community project or take up some form of voluntary work? You may have specific needs or simply wish to extend your circle.

Whatever it is you are looking for, you have to overcome your fears and anxieties about taking further any plans to increase your social connections. Do you feel uncomfortable and anxious? Are you afraid of being hurt or rejected? Or perhaps you lack the motivation to get things moving in the right direction. Think about why you have resisted meeting new people and what underlies your concerns. Perhaps you are afraid of being rejected, hurt or embarrassed or maybe it is simply a fear of the unknown. Are these fears real or are they just symptoms of your social anxiety? What have you got to lose by reaching out to other people?

To help you get out there and meet new people, here are some suggestions you could try:

- Join an evening class to meet people with similar interests and learn a new skill or hobby at the same time.
- Host a 'party plan' event as an excuse to invite friends and acquaintances round. This sort of party is more structured and less intimidating than a purely social event.
- Join a forum, group or chat room on the internet to meet like-minded people.
- Join a 'personals' or a dating website to meet new friends and

romantic partners in a non-threatening way. This is a great resource for introverts and anyone who is shy as you can take things at your own pace – but be careful that the internet does not become a substitute for meeting people in real face-to-face social situations.

- Get chatting to people who you see every day but don't necessarily have a conversation with. Perhaps you smile and nod at the same person every day at the railway station or bus stop – be the first to break the ice and get chatting. You never know, it could lead to a rewarding new friendship.
- Get your friends to introduce you to people they know. Small informal dinner parties or a get-together for drinks can be a great way to get to know new people and you will still have your trusted friends there for moral support.
- Find an excuse to chat to people at work. Lots of new friendships and even romances start at work because you have more time to get to know each other.
- Look up old friends who have fallen by the wayside. Perhaps you could use the internet to track them down.
- Join clubs where you will meet people with similar interests. Try joining the local gym or health club and get fit at the same time.
- Start going to new places with your existing friends. It might be good for everyone to meet new people and extend their social network.

Once you start looking, there are lots of ways you can meet new people. One of the best is to join social or community groups that are devoted to the same interests that you already have or would like to nurture.

Conversation worries

Shy people worry about starting a conversation because of the fear of rejection or embarrassment, but the secret of making successful conversation is not what you say but whether you come across as warm and caring. Provided you make a sincere and genuine effort to communicate you will make a good impression. Remember that conversation and communication involves more than words; it involves body language, facial expressions such as smiling and eye contact. When you greet people with an open posture, a big smile and lots of eye contact, you will come across as friendly and approachable, and that is half the battle won.

Starting a conversation

So what should you say to get a conversation going? Actually, you can talk about practically any sort of trivia. You can even resort to that great British preoccupation with the weather! Small talk is just that – non-threatening and impersonal chitchat that gives people the opportunity to size each other up and provides a transition into more meaningful conversation.

When appropriate, you can begin to discuss topics and feelings not normally covered during small talk. Show an interest in the other person, ask about her work, hobbies and experiences and keep the spotlight on her. People generally enjoy talking about themselves and you can maintain a successful conversation simply by listening and asking questions to prompt them into doing most of the talking. Again it might help to write down some ideas beforehand. You might have a plan in your mind of the sort of questions you can fall back on in a general conversation with anybody. The main thing is to keep a positive and friendly attitude and to show a genuine interest in the other person.

Give a smile!

Give someone a special smile. Researchers have recorded dozens of different types of smiles, ranging from the tight-lipped smile of someone who's been caught out in a lie to the beautifully natural spontaneous smile of a baby. Smiles can be warm, cold, fake or genuine and we subconsciously detect these different types of smiles as part of our non-verbal communication skills. Shy people are often very good at reading these sorts of signals – have a go at your own research when 'people watching' and see how many different types of smile you can identify. When you are chatting to people, make sure your smile is genuine, warm and responsive. Genuine smiles overflow into your eyes and will make the recipient feel that your special smile is just for them. What a great way to start a conversation!

Tips for conversation

Here are some more conversation tips:

- Maintain good eye contact. Just as there are different types of smile, eye contact can vary from a quick glance to the intense stare of an opponent. When you look intently at someone, it increases their heartbeat and releases adrenalin-like chemicals into the bloodstream (the same sort of response occurs when you start to fall in love). Show interest in someone by maintaining soft, comfortable and responsive eye contact.
- Turn towards the person you are chatting with. When we are interested in someone and what they have to say, we turn towards them. Sometimes this is very subtle, such as just a foot pointing towards someone in a group, but when we are engaged in conversation we turn our whole body towards the person we are talking to. When you show interest in someone in this way, they will warm to you instantly.
- To help you project the right body language when you meet someone, imagine that this person is an old friend. Use this mental trick to get your body to start a subconscious chain reaction which will soften your eyebrows, adjust your smile, position your body and fine-tune your whole body language to make sure your first impression gives off the right signals. Research has shown that if people subconsciously sense that someone likes them from their body language, they express higher respect and affection for that person and will often end up genuinely liking them.
- Be aware of the body language and reactions of the person you are with. Just as people can read your body language, you can read theirs. Does this person seem interested in what you have to say, with an open body posture, good eye contact and a genuine smile, or does he seem uninterested? If people start turning or stepping away from you, looking away for long periods or seem tense, it's time to change the subject. When you are shy, you are generally supersensitive to the moods of other people anyway, so you should have no trouble reading body language.
- Don't fidget. Fidgeting gives off the wrong signals and sets off a negative gut feeling in the recipient. People who are lying are

emotionally aroused and tend to fidget, so whether you really are lying or simply fidgeting because you are nervous, the people you are with will be suspicious of you because they will not be able to tell the difference. Professional communicators know this and consciously subdue any signals that could be misconstrued. They avoid scratching itches, rubbing their noses, twiddling with their hair, loosening their collar when it's hot or any sort of fidgeting because they know it undermines their credibility.

- Try to match the mood of the person you are with. I'm sure you've experienced the discomfort of mismatched moods – when you're late and rushing to get somewhere and someone interrupts you with a long rambling story about themselves, or when you're dog tired and simply want to relax, while somebody is overexcited and starts firing questions at you. Stop and tune in for a moment; it will help you communicate and empathize with people better.

- Have some answers ready. People engaged in conversation with someone new will inevitably ask certain questions, such as 'where are you from?' and 'what do you do?'. Instead of answering with a short sentence, have a more elaborate answer ready. Learn some interesting facts about your area and practise talking in more detail about your occupation, hobbies and interests. When you reciprocate with the same questions, the person you are talking to is more likely to elaborate their answer too and they will think that *you're* a great conversationalist.

- Be ready. Brainstorm around these inevitable questions that people refer to so that you can keep the conversation going. Instead of just asking someone what they do and where they live, keep probing and asking for more detail about their work and their lives to get them talking about themselves. Ask if there are any nice parks in their area, what the shopping is like and if there are any good restaurants. The trick is to expand and diversify each topic of conversation. Before you know it you will be happily chatting away and your nerves will be forgotten.

- Look for conversation clues. Listen out for the topics your conversation partner is most interested in. For example if you comment on the rain and she replies, 'Yes, but the garden *needs* a drop of rain', perhaps she likes gardening and plants. This is your clue to pursue the topic. You could say 'Oh, do you like gardening?' and get her to tell you all about her hobby.

- When someone is obviously enthusiastic about a topic, keep him talking about it. Show that you are interested and want to learn more.
- Keep the conversation positive and keep your skeletons in the closet until you know someone much better.
- Keep up to date with news and current affairs. When you know what's going on in the world, you always have something to talk about and can join in more confidently when other people are discussing items in the news. Try keeping a notebook where you jot down interesting stories from newspapers, radio or the internet.

The secret of successful conversation is really to show interest in the person you are talking to. When you get people talking about themselves and their interests it not only keeps the conversation going, it also makes it easy for people to like you. Not only that but it gives you time to settle down, quell your nerves and focus away from your own self-consciousness.

Dating and finding romance

Most of us would like to have someone special in our lives, but getting out there to find someone can be a bit overwhelming if you're a shy or introverted single. Dating can be exciting and fun but if you are shy, it can also be nerve-racking, scary and rather daunting. However, dating is an important process that helps you to get to know someone so that you can decide if they are right for you. By gradually getting to know someone, one date at a time, you get to see that person in different situations and you learn about how he or she responds and reacts to life events. You get to know the person's character and learn about his or her strengths and weaknesses. Is she honest, always acting with integrity, or do you have trouble trusting her? Is he kind and compassionate or angry and resentful? Does she blame others or does she take responsibility for herself? Does he need constant attention or is he self-sufficient? These sorts of questions are important to help you to clarify whether someone is right for you and dating is the best way to find out.

Use dating as a way of evaluating your compatibility with someone and also to see how your feelings develop over time with a potential partner. Do you have meaningful conversations? Do you feel comfortable with one another during the silences? Do you feel compatible intellectually? Do you feel invigorated or jaded in his or her company? Do you feel controlled or overwhelmed? It is important to take the necessary time to get to know someone.

Tips for dating

Here are some more dating tips:

- If you are meeting someone for the first time, whether it is a first date or a new friend, make the first meeting short with a pre-arranged start and stop time – perhaps for coffee or a drink – and make it a location where you can easily leave if and when you want to.
- Meet somewhere public and tell a friend where you are going and who you are meeting – always be safe.
- Wear something comfortable and appropriate. Dress in a way that expresses your personality – don't force yourself to be someone that you're not.
- Write down some ideas and topics for conversation. When you are nervous, your mind can easily go blank. Don't worry if this happens to you; it is normal and happens to everyone! If it's a problem, you can excuse yourself and have a quick look at your notes for inspiration.
- Don't worry about feeling nervous. People can be quite flattered when someone is a little nervous around them – they must be having an impact! And don't forget, the other person may be just as nervous as you. Try to focus on him or her rather than on your own self-consciousness!
- Don't feel responsible for the whole date. It takes two people to have a conversation.
- Have fun! Dating doesn't have to be serious.

Don't forget that you don't have to be a wonderful conversation-alist to win someone's heart – you just have to be yourself. Two people will either be compatible or they won't, and this simplicity can be quite liberating. Take a philosophical view of the process of dating and realize that your whole relationship won't flounder because you were nervous or couldn't think of something witty to say on the first couple of dates. The principles of attraction and compatibility are far more fundamental than that.

People are subconsciously attracted to certain types. Physical attraction might be what interests both partners to begin with but as two people get to know each other better, character, personality and compatibility are what determine whether the relationship develops into a romance or loving relationship.

Finding someone special

Successful romantic relationships are based on friendship, respect and passion. True friendship involves meeting one another's deep emotional needs for understanding, acceptance, affection and appreciation. Friendship also involves trust, and behaving in a way that is worthy of someone's trust. Respect is usually perceived as a measure of someone's self-reliance and independence. We are drawn to people who are strong and emotionally independent and often repelled by those who are overly dependent, possessive or 'clingy'. Passion is the fire that kindles a romantic relationship and distinguishes romantic love from the love we feel for our friends and family.

Compatibility

Generally speaking, shy and sensitive people tend to be more compatible with other shy, sensitive people. People who both have sensitive, reflective natures are naturally suited to each other. They are inclined to understand one another, share similar interests and find it easier to develop a close, intimate relationship. If you are introverted as well are shy, you will have inward-flowing energy and tend to be reflective, vulnerable to criticism and have a need for privacy. Shy introverts are generally comfortable with their own company, they value their inner life and can happily retreat into their own thoughts. They have a few close friends and acquaintances and tend to maintain long-term relationships with just a few special people. Shy introverts enjoy spending time at home in quiet pursuits such as reading, writing, watching films and documentaries or listening to music.

From research conducted by Alexander Avila, male shy introverts are better suited to shy introverted women while female shy introverts are compatible with introverts and shy extrovert partners. He found that while shy women are able to cope with an extrovert partner, male introverts had more problems when paired with female extroverts, largely due to the way men and women are socialized and the attitudes of society. Men are traditionally seen as more outspoken and assertive in relationships and introvert men can feel overwhelmed and intimidated by a strong-minded and outspoken extrovert woman. However, this is not to say that these relationships can *never* work.

Shy extroverts have the sensitivity and reflection of shy introverts but get their energy from socializing and being with other people. Shy extroverts can benefit greatly from having an extrovert partner to help them get out and socialize with people.

Making the right choice

Whatever physical or personality type you are drawn to in a romantic partner, it is important to find someone you can trust and respect; someone who will allow you to be yourself and help you to reach your full potential. Make sure you find someone who is right for you and take plenty of time to evaluate your relationship. You can often be lonelier in an unfulfilling or destructive relationship than you would be if you stayed alone. Here are some tips for finding the right relationship:

- Look for someone with sterling character who treats you well. Avoid people who are manipulative or dishonest and look for people who are considerate and respectful and who act with integrity. Character is one of the most essential qualities you should look for in a lifelong partner. Character is a manifestation of our inner self. It is everything a person stands for, the values he or she lives by and the morals which guide the way he or she treats you and everyone else. Don't confuse character with personality. Someone can have a sparkling personality on the outside but a rotten character on the inside. Look for someone who is committed to growing and improving himself or herself; is emotionally open and in touch with his or her feelings; is mature and takes responsibility for himself or herself; acts with integrity and is trustworthy; has high self-esteem and can look after himself or herself (how can anyone love you if they can't love themselves?); has a positive attitude to life and looks for decency and goodness in the world.

- Remember that your partner needs as much love and reassurance as you do. Everyone is secretly scared of rejection and of being hurt by the one they love. If you like someone, let them know. If someone is right for you, they'll be flattered and excited that you like them – and if not, then you won't be wasting your time on someone who does not reciprocate your feelings.
- Be yourself. Don't change yourself to fit in with what you think your partner wants you to be. This sort of behaviour is not only dishonest and prevents you from being spontaneous, but relationships based on manipulative behaviour are doomed to failure. Be honest about your feelings.
- Avoid people who 'play games'. Emotional games are based on deception, secrecy and competition and are not a healthy way to build a good relationship. Your sensitive, reflective nature should be good at detecting people who don't ring true. Just avoid them. There are lots of genuine, intelligent, well-balanced people out there who could be right for you.
- Find out about someone before you get too involved. It might not seem very romantic, but you can avoid a lot of heartache by stepping back now and again and looking at your relationship in an objective way. You wouldn't buy a house without making sure it was a suitable place to build a home – make sure the person is right for you to build a relationship with. Ask questions about her family background and the sort of relationships she had with her family; past love relationships and why they didn't work; her attitudes about love and commitment; her personal and professional aspirations; her philosophy of life; her ethics, values and morals and the lessons she has learned from life.
- Pay attention to the warning signs of possible problems and don't be blinded by love. Listen to your intuition. When you feel that something is 'not quite right' about someone, then you may be heading for trouble.
- Make sure your partner is *really* available and that he is not

married or involved in another relationship. This might seem obvious, but also includes people who are with a partner but are 'planning to leave'; with a partner but say they don't love him or her any more; with a partner but say they are only staying for the children; with a partner but not having sex any more; with someone who knows about you but says it's all right; or who have just left someone but are unsure of their feelings about it. You can only create a healthy relationship with someone who is available both physically and emotionally.

• Judge people on *who they are*, not what they can offer you. Don't evaluate people by their money, lifestyle, prestige or career and don't fall in love with a person's potential. Money is not a substitute for a happy, intimate and fulfilling relationship. Look for someone you can love based on what is in their heart and soul.

You should not focus simply on 'getting a partner' but on getting the right partner for you. Once you have found that person, the priority is to create a healthy, loving and respectful relationship, rather than simply working towards marriage or another form of commitment. Develop things at your own pace. Once you have a healthy, balanced relationship, the commitment will occur naturally.

15

Coping with more serious difficulties

It is not unusual for people who are shy to suffer other problems at the same time. Depression, panic attacks, anxiety about other things in life and problems with being assertive are some of the difficulties that can go alongside shyness and social anxiety. Some people may use alcohol for 'Dutch courage'. While the odd drink in social company can help you to relax, it can sometimes become too much of a habit.

Treating shyness and social phobia

Some clinicians may turn to drugs such as antidepressants, which may also reduce anxiety, as a method of treating severe cases of social phobia. However, by far the most effective and permanent treatment for shyness, social anxiety and even severe social phobia is *Cognitive Behavioural Therapy*, or CBT.

Research suggests that social anxiety is due to negative and irrational beliefs about oneself. Shy people overestimate the potential threat of a social situation and underestimate their ability to cope with the problem. Faulty thought processes and a misguided internal dialogue cause these irrational beliefs, and psychologists argue that by changing the way shy people think, one can also change the way they feel. CBT programmes teach shy people how to identify, test and discard irrational beliefs in favour of a more effective and useful way of thinking about their social lives. When shy people try new techniques and begin to experience success in their social interactions, their attitudes, feelings and thought processes also change and generate increased self-confidence.

Treatment is designed to focus on challenging and changing negative beliefs. This is done by getting people to gather evidence that contradicts their negative thinking patterns, often by keeping a diary of their feelings and social behaviour. Another useful method

is for people to think through the worst possible outcome and go
through a process of thinking 'what if ...' with a variety of negative, worst-case scenarios to illustrate how unrealistic their fears
are. Once negative thoughts and beliefs are challenged, tested and
disputed, people can substitute more positive thoughts and beliefs
about themselves.

A typical eight-week CBT programme will encourage you to
begin making a record of your thoughts in social situations, and
to monitor your negative thoughts and beliefs and how you felt
on each occasion. Your therapist will then encourage you to challenge these thoughts and beliefs and substitute them for positive
ones. After several weeks, you may be asked to practise these
new techniques in a moderately difficult social situation before
going on to practise starting and maintaining conversations with
friends, acquaintances and strangers. At each stage you will discuss
your progress with your therapist, or with other clients in a CBT
group, and plan each stage carefully. As you become aware of the
thought processes that are holding you back, you will progress to
practise being more assertive in several different social situations.
Throughout the programme, you will be encouraged to plan your
own timetable of change. CBT can be very effective but it does rely
on the motivation of the person and her ability to take responsibility for her own behaviour. Many of the techniques discussed in
this book are based on CBT.

Helping yourself

If you want to try a self-help approach to overcoming shyness and
social anxiety, work through this book and try out the ideas and
techniques that appeal to you. Here are some more tips to help you
plan a self-help treatment programme:

- Start a journal of your feelings, both generally on a day-to-day
  level and specifically with reference to how you feel during
  social interactions. Just record how you feel for a few weeks.
  For example, 'I feel silly and self-conscious'; 'I feel embarrassed
  that I said the wrong thing'; 'I'll never be able to face them
  again'.
- Develop your journal. Begin to identify what triggers your

feelings and try to challenge your beliefs. For example, 'I felt silly and self-conscious when John teased me about my presentation. I thought it was because I said the wrong thing but maybe it's because John likes me and he thought that teasing me and making me laugh would help me to feel less nervous ... I thought I'd never be able to face them again but everyone has been kind to me since my presentation, so it couldn't have been that bad'.

- Plan to push yourself a little more each week. For example, you could plan to start a conversation with the lady who always smiles at you at the railway station. Visualize in your mind how you will approach her and what you will say. Think about ways you can keep a conversation going.

- Start to be a little more assertive with people who tend to take advantage of you. For example, instead of automatically agreeing to babysit for your neighbour as you usually do whenever she asks, say no – or at the very least say you will have to think about it on this occasion. Try out some of the other tips in this book to help you become more assertive.

- Practise the techniques to help you increase self-esteem and self-confidence.

- Think realistically. Thinking positively is important but you have to allow for the possibility that life is sometimes difficult. Other people take advantage of us and we are not always welcomed into a social circle as we would hope. Realistic thinking gets you to weigh up all the evidence and come to a logical conclusion about the truth. It's normal to feel angry, sad or anxious when things go wrong but it is important to realize that these feelings will change when your circumstances improve or when you challenge and replace faulty beliefs.

- Remember that your feelings are directly caused by your attitudes, beliefs or thoughts about a situation, not by the situation itself.

- Extreme thoughts or beliefs lead to extreme emotions. For example, if you believe that you will *never* be able to cope with speaking to a group of people and that you will completely fall apart if your boss asks you to contribute at a meeting, your thoughts and beliefs will create sheer panic. However, if you tone down your thoughts or beliefs it will lead to less extreme emotions. Believe that maybe you *could* cope with speaking to a group of people at work that you know well. You may be nervous about it, but you *would* cope and you *wouldn't* fall apart.

- Practise focusing your attention on other people rather than concentrating on your inner turmoil during social interactions. This may have to be a conscious effort at first, but soon it will become second nature and a very effective coping mechanism.
- Take it all one step at a time. Don't push yourself to achieve too much too soon but formulate a plan and set yourself goals to achieve within a specific and realistic timescale.
- Remember that as your pattern of thinking changes, you create new neural networks, effectively restructuring your brain. You can help to make these new ways of thinking a permanent part of your life simply by repeating and reinforcing your desired thoughts and behaviour.
- Have fun and think about all the benefits of changing your behaviour. If you can overcome your anxiety about being with other people you will open up a whole new world of exciting opportunities – what are yours?

If you have tried the ideas in this book as a way to make changes in your life, yet you still feel overwhelmed and unable to cope with your problems alone, you should see your GP for a physical checkup and ask to be referred for some counselling or appropriate psychological therapy. Sometimes we need help to get on top of things and to understand the root of our problems. Don't suffer alone – get the help you need.

Finally ...

As you begin to try out the ideas in this book, you may feel a little overwhelmed or daunted at the prospect of making changes, even though that is what you desperately want to achieve. Remember that everyone, at times, can get themselves worked up into a frenzy about problems and concerns that are really not that important and soon sort themselves out. Try to get some perspective on your problems. See your social anxiety as just part of your life – it is not your *whole* life.

Each time you come up against another setback or problem, ask yourself whether it will matter a year from now. The chances are that 12 months from now, it will be fairly irrelevant and unimportant. Think back to a year ago and try to remember a situation that was similar in magnitude to the problem you are facing at the moment. How do you feel about it now? Do you think that the energy you expended on worrying about it at the time was justified? Try to create an objective distance between *you* and your problems.

Avoid focusing on your imperfections and your limitations. Nobody in this world is perfect but when you are always focused on what is wrong, you often miss what is right and good in your life. While it is great to work on your problems and to make desired changes in your life, don't forget to enjoy and appreciate what you already have. Think of and appreciate all the wonderful things you have and be proud of everything you have achieved in your life so far. Being shy can be very debilitating, but it also means you possess wonderful qualities within your personality. Be glad that you are blessed with such a sensitive, caring and understanding nature and embrace *who* you are – the world needs people like you.

With all good wishes on your journey towards a confident new you …

Resources

Useful addresses

National Phobics' Society
Zion Community Resource Centre
339 Stretford Road
Hulme
Manchester M15 4ZY
Tel.: 08444 775 774
Fax: 0161 226 7727
Website: www.phobics-society.org.uk
Email: info@phobics-society.org.uk

Provides help with anxiety and panic attacks.

Royal College of Psychiatrists
17 Belgrave Square
London SW1X 8PG (send an SAE addressed to the Information Service)

Has a free leaflet on social phobia, which can also be found at <www. rcpsych.ac.uk/mentalhealthinformation/mentalhealthproblems/ anxietyphobias/socialphobia.aspx>.

Triumph Over Phobia
PO Box 3760
Bath BA2 3WY
Tel.: 0845 600 9601
Website: www.topuk.org
Email: info@topuk.org

Runs a national network of self-help groups, and its website gives help and advice about phobias.

Books

Avila, Alexander, *The Gift of Shyness: Embrace Your Shy Side and Find Your Soul Mate*. Simon & Schuster, New York, 2002.
Butler, Gillian, *Overcoming Social Anxiety and Shyness: A Self-help Guide Using Cognitive Behavioural Techniques*. Robinson, London, 1999.
Fennell, Melanie, *Overcoming Low Self-esteem*. Robinson, London, 1999.

Laney, Marti Olsen, *The Introvert Advantage: How to Thrive in an Extrovert World*. Workman Publishing, New York, 2002.

Lowndes, Leil, *How to Talk to Anyone: Ninety-two Little Tricks for Big Success in Relationships*. Thorsons, London, 1999.

Lyle, Jane, *Body Language: Read the Hidden Codes and Maximize Your Potential*. Guild Publishing, London, 1990.

Matthews, Andrew, *Making Friends: A Guide to Getting Along with People*. Media Masters, Singapore, 1990.

Muir, Alice, *Make Your Sensitivity Work for You*. Sheldon Press, London, 2006.

Rapee, Ronald M., *Overcoming Shyness and Social Phobia: A Step-by-step Guide*. Rowman & Littlefield, Oxford, 2004.

Roet, Brian, *The Confidence To Be Yourself*. Piatkus, London, 1999.

Searle, Ruth, *The Thinking Person's Guide to Happiness*. Sheldon Press, London, 2007.

Webber, Christine, *Get the Self-esteem Habit*. Hodder, London, 2002.

Websites

BBC Health

www.bbc.co.uk/health/conditions/mental_health/index.shtml

A mental health website with information about many mental health problems and their treatments.

Other websites

www.anapsys.co.uk/Disorders/social_anxiety.htm
www.dontcallmeshy.com/Welcome.html
www.overcoming shyness.com
www.shyandfree.com
www.shyness.co.uk
www.shynesscurve.com/curve/index.asp
www.sussex.ac.uk/Users/ss216/

Index